# *Assorted Selfscriptings 1964-1985*

Eugene Stelzig

2015
Milne Library

©2015 Eugene Stelzig

ISBN: 978-1-942341-12-3

*This work is licensed under the Creative Commons Attribution-ShareAlike 4.0 International License. To view a copy of this license, visit http://creativecommons.org/licenses/by-sa/4.0/.*

You are free to:

*Share—copy and redistribute the material in any medium or format*

*Adapt—remix, transform, and build upon the material*

*The licensor cannot revoke these freedoms as long as you follow the license terms.*

Under the following terms:

*Attribution—You must give appropriate credit, provide a link to the license, and indicate if changes were made. You may do so in any reasonable manner, but not in any way that suggests the licensor endorses you or your use.*

*ShareAlike—If you remix, transform, or build upon the material, you must distribute your contributions under the same license as the original.*

*Published by Milne Library*

*State University of New York at Geneseo,*

*Geneseo, NY 14454*

# Praise for *Assorted Selfscriptings*

A record of warmth and wisdom, informed by sly wit, passionate compassion, and a sure ear for the music of language and the voice of the spirit—this is the poetry of Eugene Stelzig.
*Stephen Behrendt, George Holmes Distinguished Professor of English, University of Nebraska, Lincoln*

I began reading Eugene Stelzig's poems back in the 1970s. The best poetry sustains us through this life, and I have found that Gene's poetry does precisely that. His lines tend not to leave you, to grow with you over time, to haunt and nurture in equal measure: "How we are leached by time, / how the wonder drains from life / through living / is the unspoken testimonial of the dead." Those lines are from Gene's magisterial "For the Death of My Mother," the longest poem (or sequence of poems) in the book—a remarkable mixture of multicultural autobiography, elegy, and confession, many lines of which are now part of *my* memory. Gene's language surprises us, enacting what he calls in one poem "the quirky demonism / of random circumstance." A "quirky demonism" captures for me the quirky Daemon that seems to inspire most Stelzig poems, where we find "we need to be broken down / to grow again, / manured by pain and joy." These peculiar and powerful poems occupy the "chill margins" that, Stelzig tells us, "are intimately mine," where "waste / space and cacti spine" are "my only crave." What demon/Daemon makes language *do* that, makes language take us into the "long winternights / that move through the soul like / unending freight trains of the dark"? The margins of many of the best poems here are indeed "chill," but poem after poem manures us with the endless wonder of "pain and joy."
*Ed Folsom, Roy J. Carver Professor of English, University of Iowa*

Stelzig's poetry, from first to last, shows a liquidity of discourse that seems to develop from a triangulation of deep intelligence, stealthy self-knowledge, and aesthetic cosmopolitanism. Lenitive and enchanting, these poems, more than most of late, bear reading up and down as well as along the lines.
*Larry H. Peer, Karl G. Maeser Professor of Comparative Literature, Brigham Young University*

In this delight-studded collection, we have the first twenty years of a lifelong love affair with poetry. In addition to considerable erudition, the author brings keen observational powers directed at both the ex-

ternal and internal worlds, as well as a refreshingly self-deprecating wit. Whether recalling his childhood in Post-War Austria, describing an encounter with a "dowsing witch," imagining hunting elephants in Western New York, or writing tender lyrics to his beloved Elsje, Eugene Stelzig brings us "September Gifts." He urges us to "let these assorted selfscriptings / disseminate beyond the margins / become and then unbecome you / let them multiply beyond / our simple mees and wees/ disperse us into other spaces and places."
*John Roche, Associate Professor of English, Rochester Institute of Technology*

Fleet of (poetic) foot, these poems of the "romantic spirit" turn and turn again with wit and wisdom alike, drawing variously from classic literature and a well-lived life to deliver their charm and insight. These are poems to make you feel the heart's beat and ache—and to make you remember the head believes it rules the heart.
*Lytton Smith, Assistant Professor of English, SUNY Geneseo*

# Preface

*Assorted Selfscriptings* is a selection from the volume(s) of poetry I wrote during roughly two decades, from the ages of twenty-one to forty-two. I found my calling as a poet during my undergraduate years at the University of Pennsylvania (1962-66), where I worked on the campus literary magazine, *The Pennsylvania Review*, which I co-edited in my senior year (we foolishly renamed it *The Handle*). Of the many poems I wrote during those years, and some of which appeared in campus publications (both under my name as well as a pseudonym), I have only included one here, "The Light Watchers," because it came to me as confirmation of my identity as a poet.

It is always difficult to make a selection from a large quantity of poetry. What I've excluded from this collection is poems that no longer resonate with me, or even speak to or for me. I've also excluded poems that are now historically dated, like a long verse satire in ottava rima on the Watergate scandal.

This collection consists, to take a title from my favorite English poet, Wordsworth (on whom I wrote my Ph.D. dissertation), of "moods of my mind." Minds change over time, and so do moods. These poems are from a past self—or more accurately, selves—that I wanted to put on the record. The states of mind recorded in them are not my present self, but perhaps a reflection of the states of mind all of us potentially pass through in life's perennial journey. As another William of English poetry, Blake, put it beautifully, "Man passes on, but States remain for Ever; he passes thro' them like a traveler who may as well suppose that the places he has passed thro' exist no more, as a Man may suppose that the States he has passed thro' Exist no more. Every thing is Eternal."

If some of these poems are embarrassingly confessional, I'm willing to shoulder that burden, reassured by the truth of that French saying, *le je est un autre* [the self is another]. These are the selves I have lived through, these are the traces or scraps or remnants—scripts and scriptings—of them. In presenting them here, almost like a dead man looking back at a substantial period of his life, I have resisted the fatal temptation that Wordsworth fell victim to: endlessly revising the poems of his earlier years in the light of the self-understanding of his later years. I have no such desire to revise or correct or rescript my younger self. To quote the Beatles, "let it be, let it be," with all its myriad and passionate imperfections on its head.

This selection from my younger years does not mean that I've stopped writing poetry. *Fool's Gold: Selected Poems of a Decade* was published by FootHills in 2008, and it is my hope that subsequent volumes in manuscript will eventually also see the light of day.

I wish to express my gratitude to SUNY Geneseo's Milne Library for making this collection available both in print and online versions, and I want to give a special "shout out" and thank you to Allison P. Brown, for taking on this project and doing the hard work of seeing it through to its completion.

# Acknowledgments

The author and publisher gratefully acknowledge the following publications in which these poems have previously appeared:

"The Light Watchers" [*The Handle*]
"Eurailer in First Class" [*Pennsylvania Gazette*]
"Pied Piper" [*The Cresset*]
"For the Death of My Mother" [*The Literary Review*]
"The Wheatland Diner" [*Indiana Writes*]
"Thirteen Ways of Looking at a Teddybear" [*Wind*]
"Living In," "Dorothy to William at Alfoxden," "Young Heine to Old Goethe in Weimar," "The Sky's the Limit," "Changes" [*Souwester*]
"Days Done," "After the Concert" [*Religious Humanism*]
"Don Jose" [*A Shout in the Street*]
"Home" [*Crab Creek Review*]
"Moving to the Country," "August Harvest" [*The Greenfield Review*]

# Contents

**Early Poems (ca. 1964-1970)**

| | |
|---|---|
| Dear Reader | *3* |
| Falstaff's Death Reported to Henry V by Ancient Pistol | *4* |
| Eurailer in First Class | *8* |
| Harvard Yard | *9* |
| The Light Watchers | *10* |
| The Roses of Great St. Mary's | *11* |
| Stringers of the Bow | *13* |
| Pauper's Grave, Arkansas, 1968 | *14* |
| My Lai Massacre (1968) | *15* |
| Home Delivery | *17* |

**A Little Fire in a Wild Field (ca. 1971-1976)**

| | |
|---|---|
| Pied Piper | *21* |
| For the Death of My Mother | *22* |
| Living In | *35* |
| The Wheatland Diner | *36* |
| Thirteen Ways of Looking at a Teddybear | *37* |
| Strange Noises | *39* |
| On My Thirtieth Birthday | *41* |
| letchworth park | *42* |
| Planting | *43* |
| December 25, 1974 | *45* |
| New Year's Day Poem (1975) | *47* |
| In King's College Library (Cambridge, June 1975) | *49* |
| Purest Form | *51* |
| The Sleep of Genius | *53* |
| Saturday Morning | *55* |
| Journeying | *56* |
| Turnpike | *64* |
| At Home | *65* |
| Day's Done | *66* |
| Marriage: Point Blank | *67* |
| Diotima to Socrates | *69* |
| Ravings of a Mad Dog Poet | *72* |
| Help | *74* |
| Somewhere | *75* |
| After the Concert | *76* |
| A Little Fire in a Wild Field | *78* |

## Paralogues (ca. 1977-1979)

| | |
|---|---|
| Dorothy to William at Alfoxden | *81* |
| Demon | *83* |
| Hungry Eyes | *84* |
| Television | *85* |
| Heidegger's *die Sprache spricht* | *86* |
| Syllables | *87* |
| Burial Grounds | *88* |
| Blackout (NYC, July 14, 1977) | *89* |
| Don Jose | *91* |
| Shadow | *92* |
| Souls of Light | *94* |
| Cross Country | *95* |
| Paralogue | *99* |
| Dream Log 1 | *100* |
| Dream Log 2 | *102* |
| Perhaps | *103* |
| Paraline | *104* |
| November Moon in Bloomington | *105* |
| Never Quite | *106* |
| Miraculous Escape | *107* |
| Luther's Blues | *108* |
| Young Heine Calls on Old Goethe in Weimar | *109* |

## Alcatraz of Hope (ca. 1980-1981)

| | |
|---|---|
| Strand of Hair | *113* |
| Lazarus | *114* |
| Foundering | *115* |
| Night Noise | *116* |
| Trite Mykonos | *118* |
| Dialect of Unknowing | *119* |
| White Wood | *121* |
| The Wall | *122* |
| Gorgon | *125* |
| Needle's Eye | *126* |
| Plastic Surgeon | *127* |
| Triumphs of Paranoia | *129* |
| Pet Phobia | *131* |
| Litany of an Expiring Mouse | *133* |
| Hands | *134* |
| Winternight Dream | *135* |
| Unbidden Guest | *137* |
| The Sky's the Limit | *138* |
| Gnostic Song | *139* |
| Changes | *141* |

| | |
|---|---:|
| Professor of Desire | *142* |
| Weed Thoughts | *144* |
| Lukewarm | *145* |
| Torn Ligament | *146* |
| Hour Test | *147* |
| Man's Best Friend | *148* |
| Waylaid | *149* |
| Centering | *150* |
| Hope | *151* |

## Moving to the Country (ca. 1982-1985)

| | |
|---|---:|
| Moving to the Country | *155* |
| Winter Hunt | *156* |
| Home | *158* |
| Bare | *159* |
| August Harvest | *160* |
| The Water Witch | *161* |
| Turning Forty | *164* |
| Inland | *165* |
| Poet Marginal | *166* |
| About Trees | *167* |
| Mimy Bird | *168* |
| Middle Ages | *169* |
| Appropriating the Land | *170* |
| Unless | *172* |
| Paths | *173* |
| Geneva Summit | *175* |
| September Gifts | *178* |

# Early Poems

*(ca. 1964–1970)*

# Dear Reader

*mon quasisemblable* if not *frère* or *sœur*
you whom i havent yet met

gimme a break

lets help each other be
let these assorted selfscriptings
disseminate beyond the margins

become and then unbecome you
let them multiply us beyond
our simple mees and wees

disperse us into other spaces and places

all books unglued all un
banished these black marks
from the white page
and dotted the blank
map of the future

let us selve ourselves
let us spread our parachutes
and float on thin air
let us by all means whistle
in the wind like the winter
starved raven on the tattered
fence let us buzz like
the honeybee in the humming hive

let us heap the bare horizon

for what i mean is
*immer nach Hause*

# Falstaff's Death Reported to Henry V by Ancient Pistol

*Scene: Winter. The English camp in France. Open country. Snow.*
*(enter Henry V and Exeter)*

*Henry*   My Lord Exeter, see the tenor of
our provisions, here set down, enforced
to the utmost article. The times are hard.
Needs must we be so. Your hand, my Lord; farewell!
*(exit Exeter)*
Who approaches now? Methinks I see
the King of Swaggerers, Ancient Pistol,
he whose banishment I lately did take off
for brave words upon the bridge at Harfleur.
What his unmanly heart lacked in timely deeds,
his brave voice, like alarum's bell tolling
in calamity, made good in the effect
on my most ragged soldiers, steeled by
such harsh music to deeds of glory.
*(enter Pistol)*
And here he comes, strangely unlike himself.
What now, Ancient Pistol? Discharge, discharge!

*Pistol*   Most noble King, I come so charged with grief
I cannot tune my tongue to note my heart.

*Henry*   This argues untimely news, sad melodies.
Wet powder, alas, ne'er fired a shot.
Come Pistol, speak thy grief or be discharged.

*Pistol*   Falstaff, the prince of flesh, is dead, my Lord.

*Henry*   Now hast thou hit me in the heart.

*Pistol*   The hulk that drained a sea of sack now lies
dry-docked on the naked shores of death.

*Henry*   Good Pistol, did 'a make a good end?
Did 'a banter with the Devil's lackeys
on his journey down to flaming Hell?
Did 'a use his scorching wit to score

                a set upon the pate of Satan?
                No? What use is wit if 'a could not use it
                to outwit the devil of his due?
                Did 'a die of the pox, or the gout, or verily of thirst?

Pistol     Good, my Lord, of thirst, of a great thirst of life.
                On's end, 'a breathed as Leviathan
                tempest-stranded, gasping in despair, long and hard.
                'A blubbered e'en as a monstrous babe,
                crying God's mercy on a rotted soul,
                and waxed feebler like to a dying fire
                consumed in his substance. His death
                had the taste of ashes. It did rain and rain.

Henry    Had he reigned his life, he would not thus
                lie sacked. Did I not warn him in his
                banishment? Still do they whisper I was
                the scourge of his age. They say the King did
                kill his heart. And how could I do other
                than I did? As Hal I reigned Prince of Eastcheap,
                but once Henry crowned, how could I countenance
                such Lords of Misrule, such infinite knaves?
                Yet I am sore grieved Falstaff hath sounded
                his last. I grieve to think what then we did,
                and turned the nights to riot, crying "hem!"
                so loud unto the world that it did shake
                the very Palace walls about the King
                my father's ears, and fretted golden
                majesty as pale as snow. Too much of that!
                We thank thee, Pistol, and we dare hope
                that Falstaff's end hath taught thee the start
                of a better life, so that thou may'st not
                betray it upon the gallows, even as
                Bardolph, who thought war's glory was in
                the pillage, and whose lanthorn face is now
                put out by death.
                Ancient Pistol, go, leave us to ourselves.

Pistol (aside)
                Leave us to ourselves? A figo for thy feigned grief!
                The Spanish figo on thy French wars! A pox upon thy God,
                thou counterfeit king, thou Styx of saintliness!
                A stinking jordan toast on reformation! I go not to
                the wars to be gelded of my life, but to be gilded o'er
                with guilders, to be armed for a noble return to England.

        And may my worst war wound be caught in a French bed.
        What, thou hast killed brave Bardolph for the robbing
        of a country church, and wouldst thyself the French
        Charles rob of crown and country? Thou base king of
        current seemliness, who treatest thine ancient familiars
        like a plague of boils to be lanced! S'blood! A French
        lance for thy troubles, says valiant, war-like Pistol!

*(exit Pistol)*

Henry *(solus)*
        Falstaff dead? What? Is it possible that
        the inimitable rogue who thought all life
        his most especial whore, should now lie
        stomach'd in the cold earth, who ne'er had flesh
        enow when quick to contain the fire
        and raging motions of his appetites?
        Alack, the counterfeit of ceaseless revelry
        is ever confounded by time's true currency.
        Those tavern days ring hollow in my ears.

*(pause)*
        Yet, what he lacked of grace, he still graced o'er with
        wit. Alas, your true wit leads but to your true grave,
        when grace is ever the high road to Heaven.
        Yes, there's a time for all things, which this royal
        parasite, this fat-stuffed Falstaff, ne'er did
        perceive. I do remember me of my wild youth;
        Sir John still feeding headstrong riot.
        Yet, he loved me as his proper son.
        I did commit a sort of regicide
        when I put on the crown and cast him off
        like a barren soil, rife with weed and waste.
        Although he was no true staff nor guide of youth
        I did love him in the heyday of his
        reign as my most prodigal father,
        and in the son-like banishment of thee,
        Sir John, I banished my heart, my youth,
        and my humanity.

*(pause)*
        Now in the bitter cold of our wars here in
        Gallia, the frost nips at my starving
        soldiers' heels like a pack of baying hounds,
        and even in the heat of victory
        my heart is not well, but waxes chill
        with the winds that rage through our weary camp,
        blowing the snow which blankets all in white.

No, Henry, all fares not well with thee, for
great Falstaff's heart lies deep in distant
England's earthy womb. Once I loved thee,
and hearing of thy death here among these
mounds of snow, I love thee anew and needs
must mourn thee as the fabled Atlantis
in the world of mirth and joy that was my youth.

Farewell, Falstaff, thou blubber whale of wit
and uproarious fellowship, thou shining
beefsteak sign of pleasure, thou great good man
of night-cheer, of sack and song and wenching.
Thou who wast a huge feeder on the earth
now feedest it, fattening all England.

*(pause)*

In the purchase of a golden crown, I lost
a goodly measure of myself. Well, an
end to such barren reckonings. Time calls,
and glory waits on the doers of God's will.
Fare thee well, old friend. Even here in the
drifting snow, even thus, I grieve,
I mourn for thee.

# Eurailer in First Class

and if youre in madrid youve got to visit the prado
stuffed with worldfamous paintings more than in the louvre
and thats saying something velasquez and goyas galore and
titians too mostly fat women the potato finger of lechery
said shakespeare and rembrandt and all the other dutch
masters even that bizarre bosch el bosco in spanish reminds me of
chagall and dont forget that illuminated fountain performs every
midnight spectacular nooo lessee thats in barcelona pronounced
barthelona well you have to go there too famous architecture
and leather goods and the jumpoff point for the balearics jewels
in the sun but overrun these days by hordes of hippyfreaks just
disgraceful girls with sweaters saying feel me up front oyes back to
madrid do go to the flamenco costs plenty but worth every peseta
and then to get away from it all el retreto famous park or was it el
retiro? water and boats and trees and lovers in rome you mustnt
of course pass up saint peters the rolls royce of western art and
in vienna the heurigen salzburger nockerln and mozartkugeln
balls you know and the view the view simply out of this world
herbert von karajan the man is musically promiscuous in a parisian
cafe was it lapaix? just a hole in the floor and you have to squat i
swear like a regular kangaroo those french so crude yet so cultured
and elegant with their bidets and the toureiffel and the academie
francaise…

# Harvard Yard

Harvard Yard is never so quintessential
as just after when it has snowed.
There it remains insulated
in a sheer fullness of white
long after the frenzied
surrounding streets
have been smutched
and the splendid snow
trampled down into a sloshy
mess knee-deep in places.

Some students en route
to library or laboratory
make a moment's pause
then hurry on.
A few professors stride by
iced with self-importance
oblivious even to

the ever-present dogs
who frolic here
racing between skeletal trees
and generally running amok
in Harvard Yard.

Statued John looks on
as he has for centuries
and wisely keeps his counsel.
The only creaturely life now

is the yelping hullaballoo
of floppy, bounding dogs

until the trees revive the spring
and advertise in full-blown green

and frizzbeeing Harvard men
watch luscious Cliffies
primly saunter by

huge with desires silent and unseen
unlike the ecstatic dogs in Harvard Yard.

# The Light Watchers

We are the light watchers
And walk past
Rock cliff river
Earth and road
We are Odysseus chainless
And unbound
We have seen all
Heard all
And prefer to play pool
In a musty midnight hall
Carnivals splinter our
Dreamless night
But we just walk and talk
And jabber
Discuss many things in detail
Quite analytic
You might say
Spectroscope every
Light and ray and rill
Perfectly objective on every side—
We prefer to look, you see
And never mind
The ride.

# The Roses of Great St. Mary's

1

The blood-red roses bloom above
the tomb-stones in Great St. Mary's
graveyard in the long, star-illumined
June nights of Cambridge.

If these graves are only rocks
with roses overgrown, then let us
rot into the ground and be as from
dust to dust and never think of roses.

When I came here two years ago
the Colleges seemed to me ancient piles
of fog-shrouded rocks rotting
into the ground in the dank winter nights.

Slowly the seasons went round
And opened out my mind.
I came to bless those medieval
miracles of stone inhabited

for centuries by the great men who
came here to learn, reflect, and feel,
forging dimension after dimension
in the possibilities of man and mind.

They died.
Here are the graves of wise men.
Their greatest tombs are their ideas,
cradles where new thought

is rocked into fruition.
Their buried bones burn
in the ground, holy fires
in a vigil of the future.

Yes, materialism will rob us all
of the whole extent of our humanity
unless we use matter only
for a new splendidness of soul.

*Early Poems*

Now, in the last incandescence of thought
In this Cambridge night of roses
I still have hopes for man not less
than these reposing in the sacred earth.

2

I sailed for New York the following day
watching the storms at sea,
watching the moon between the clouds
cut a trail of gold across the water.

From the deck of the ship I saw
The rose-stars dance on the waves.
To constellate the mind I thought
in the night there on the sea.

The ship glided into the rust-red
smoke-stained dawn of the new world harbor.
I thought of Great St. Mary's graveyard
and walked away from roses for many a day.

# Stringers of the Bow

Young Master Tell, son of William,
famed artist of the great strong bow,
had an apple shot neatly off the top
of his head by his cool-aiming progenitor.

Tell's son, in a paroxysm of fear
when he felt the arrow whir
and breathe on his hair
as it split the fruit

felt an instant proximity with the dead
yet lived to see many more
apple seasons green
with leaf and fruit.

The poet too is a stringer
of the great strong bow.
He aims carefully,
and runs a grave risk

for he's both master archer
and master target.
He's got to take unflinching aim
and needs must keep a cool head when

letting fly the feathered shaft.

# Pauper's Grave, Arkansas, 1968

One man's body was too long
so we had to cut off his head
to make him fit. Later we
didn't use no coffins.
I don't know how many we
shot, you lose count.
I helped out once on a cool
March morning when they buried
three cons. We always said
they was tryin' to escape.
We dug a pit, turning up
the black earth with shovels
in a fallow field near the prison.
We piled in the bodies and
quickly threw the earth back
in when it begun to rain.
Later we planted the field
with corn. In the summer
when it had shot up full
and tall, the prisoners
harvested the crop, cutting
and binding in the hot sun.

# My Lai Massacre (1968)

Son My, My Lai
American soldiers
are murdering today.

When words fail Son My
the camera eye
will testify:
women's, men's bodies,
babies'
tortured into the grotesque definition
of instant gunfire massacre.
Tumbled helter skelter
into a ditch gorged and
swollen with death.
This butchery is ours:
Son My, My Lai
inhuman men have come here today.

A toddler runs from a blazing hut,
his chest gushing blood.
His puzzled terrified
four years' eyes
are sleep murdering.

Because because is an
obscenity here,
because our explanations
do not explain
the American dream is a nightmare.

Because of Son My My Lai
America is murdering today.
Silent eyes like stone
O now bear witness.

Manners do not make humanity,
but kindness does
which is true innocence
won by self-restraint and knowledge
from the ferocity
of our feral nature.

In this wilderness the mind
undone by a vertigo of outrage
falls into the great silence of the age.
Son My, Son My My Lai
the inhuman men
are murdering today.

# Home Delivery

What was left of him after
the jungle fire fight
was stuffed into a plastic bag,
named, numbered, labeled and mailed home,
shattered flesh and bone coffined in
refrigerated metal hurtling
through alien skies.

He never believed the patriotic lies
which sent him to his fire death.

Now, after an officious delivery
to his parents' city, and during
the droning service recited
by the ceremonious priest

He cannot see his father curse
nor hear his mother cry and moan
because she may not look upon
him hidden under the flag-afflicted
coffin like some dismembered beast.

She isn't sure it is her own,
she cannot see,
she isn't sure of anything.

And so she sobs because
she cannot hear the priest,
she sobs and chokes on her breath

Because this metal-enmeshed things
which once moved in her womb
is now more dead than death.

*From*

# A Little Fire in a Wild Field

*(ca. 1971-1976)*

# Pied Piper

The Pied Piper was playing in the square,
the rats were grooving in broad daylight
stoned by the set. "Outta sight!" they
shrilled, "man, can that cat ever blow!"
The fat burghers of Hamelin
smirked in relief as they saw
the rats in transports at
the Piper's unearthly tracks.
The ratpack whirred, eyes agog:
"wow, the greatest riff we ever
heard! man, let's follow that
man!" O the Pied Piper piped
such a set as never yet was
heard in Hamelin, the rats
went sheer crazy, the kids
were as silent as stones.

The Pied Man forced his heart
out all down the streets of
Hamelin, the rats padded behind
in droves, mind-blown,

and the little kids traipsed
along on tiptoes,
mesmerized.
In the guildhall of Hamelin
the fat burghers smirked,
the old women slapped their
sides, rolled their eyes,
and crooned, "that'll
fix them."

# For the Death of My Mother

*"Und wenn der Mensch in seiner Qual verstummt,*
*Gab mir ein Gott, zu sagen, wie ich leide."*

**1. The Graveyard by the Lake**

Glossing the epitaphs,
deciphering faded or crusted ones,
we came on a Sunday afternoon

my mother and I
with flowers and smiles
to grandfather's tomb

in the graveyard by the lake at Zell am See

where now she herself lies
bedded down for eternity
there in the ground washed

by the clean mountain air and rain.

We were neither gay nor sad then,
but peaceful, light of heart,
like the stars at dawn,

silent

blessing the dead,
carrying bunches of asters and roses
in homage from the garden at home.

How we are leached by time,
how the wonder drains from life
through living
is the unspoken testimonial of the dead.

Blessed are these dead,
for here the firs and pines whisper in the sun,
blessed are they,
for here the lake-waters lap a peaceful shore.

So fortunate are they
on this golden day
of spring.

## 2. Documentary 1

I was born in Bischofshofen,
Bishop's Court, that is, Austria,
in August nineteen-hundred and forty-three.
Shortly my family moved to Taxenbach
and then to Zell am See
the village of my heart
very near the Grossglockner
and the majestic range of the high alps.

I remember the foreign occupying troops,
the American G.I.'s walking the town
which I considered home,
with their clumsy generosity
to children—candy, fruit,
and gum—and the sheepish
grins with which they
approached the women.
They had steak, and we polenta;
they looked at us, I think,
as a sort of white nigger,
kindly for the most part,
but condescending,
these paternal victors
who were uncle-tommed.

At home my mother would weep
the nights and days
out of countenance,
the schizophrenic leer
was etched on Christ's face
in the smoke-stained corner
of the kitchen, Christ
so pale and frail
in the shadows of the room.

My mother clung to me
like a glacier witch
with black disheveled hair,
with deviled eyes glowing

in the darkness when
they came to take her away:
what words from her lips cut
into my eyes
what fear shattered my head
when she crushed me to her heart
in her unending frantic plea:
*Eugen, bitte, bitte, lass sie nicht…!*
Oh don't let them!
the prayer gurgling from her throat
like black blood:

I drowned in the words of hell
in the sunshine of my childhood
on the broken throne of my days

yet grew up somehow
to live this circus show
as best I could
in and out of various cages of the soul.

What countries I have been—
Austria, France, England,
but chiefly U.S.A.—
I have gone beyond
so that I'm all of these and none,
although the language of my heart
has become for better or worse
English.

**Documentary 2**

After I almost committed suicide in Somerville success-
fully half by design and half by accident
the first thing I saw when
I went outside was
a Cadillac hearse driving by,
and the second
a huge rat sauntering
self-assuredly across the road.
He jumped up and watched me from a porch
as I, incredulous, went by.
Not wanting to be superstitious,
but feeling rather odd
I forced a laugh

and put it down
to the quirky demonism
of random circumstance.

### 3. Memorials

My childhood is a dark forest
with occasional clearings of memory.
Strange forms glide between the trees
in the crepuscular light,
stranger creatures yet avoid
the beaten tracks of introspection.

Skiing through the quiet wood
one Sunday afternoon in early spring
alone, I paused
and looked at the sunlight
burnishing the deep green firs
with golden lustre.
It was very still,
and the more I looked into the silence,
the more silent it grew.
The undertone of snow
sifted by the breeze
focused the silence,
and confirmed what now
I consciously know:

Nature, no matter how beautiful,
is always another.
It may tell us things, but
on the whole we're strictly on our own
and must make do with what we've got
within.

Here in my hands a snapshot
of you I took two summers ago
on my last visit to Austria.
Your face is pale
and distorted with age prematurely.

It looks fissured with grief
and weary of too many days.
You suffered much, I know,
but still your smile sometimes managed

to shine through
the gloomy cave of your sorrow.

Those who do not suffer
*sind gar keine Menschen,*
gay bubbles suddenly pricked
by death,
while appalling sorrow fuses the soul
into a fierce integrity forever.

Your face like a gnarled root
Is its own testimony
which the pellucid camera eye
could do no more
than simply record.

The furrows of your brow show so well
the shadows of your cheek tell
what these words cannot.

### 4. Words

Everybody's at them.
Now the word is violated everywhere
except in a few minds
which hang in the balance isolated.

With Adolf Hitler the beast
came back full strong again,
tearing the flesh of language
with its greedy fangs.
Begin only by violating the word
and you always end up
by ravaging humanity.

The calculated passionate misuse of language
is not merely a literary crime.
In no time
propaganda murders the mind
and then the man.
The beast, we know, will devour
both word and man,
but only through the subtle spell
of the word may the beast

be charmed, turning to
the tuneful harmony of numbers,

Prosper's airy song upon the waters.

**5. Past Time**

I can remember much,
and much I have forgotten:

the bell-like gentian, bluest of blue,
swaying in the wind high on a mountain slope

a drunken fool urinating on a wall
with self-congratulatory laughter

the blooming heart of the alps
where the sun sings all summer long
freckling and fretting the glaciers away

gaudy inane tourists trooping the streets
extensions of cameras and binoculars

the summer lake bordered
for a five-year old by a jungle
of reeds among which to dream
the time away all alone

and my mother in the hospital
in Salzburg
so near yet so far
the dreary endless wards like railroad tunnels

fish belly up polluting the shore
*edelweiss* sealed in glass expensively
for the city-folk
fake crystal cages of mountainglory

breaking a leg the first time on skates…
the *foehn*, lukewarm, roaring down the alps,
fretting, irritable, from a vast distance
to blast your cheek
cable-cars suspended on silver threads

above seas of snow,
glittering specks in the sun

Christ in the shadows

Children of the war,
blighted in the seed of our youth
by a world in whose making we had no say,
still we were the sun's own ragged crew,
hardly touched by the guilt and despair
of foreign occupation which lay
with the weight of death
upon the grownups' nightmare world.

Our ignorance was our blessing
in this lean decade
of a crazy century.
Hunger, what was not hunger
that was not earth or sky
or flashing lakeside green,
that was not mother and father
and way of the world?

These are things I partly remember
and was told partly later,
truths colored perhaps by fabulation.

Bartering with farmers:
a cackling gaggle of geese
in the mired farmyard
crowding in on me and nibbling at my legs
it seems with ferocious clacking
and I cling to you in sheer terror.

The hearts of these farmers on their rocky
mountain slopes were harder by far
than the family jewels
you brought for bread
and eggs and butter,
mother mine.

They gaged their greed
according to our need,
flint-dry, shrewd misers,
peasant crafty, wizened.

Man lives not by bread alone,
but without it
sometimes he dies.

When the Americans came
the soldiers requisitioned our home,
and played with your prized sewing machine,
and broke it, of course.
You cried bitterly, for
it was the last piece
of complex regularity
however paltry
that finally went smash
and no one knew
how life would go on.

I was only two then,
and do not remember
except what you and Papa
told me later.

>
> *o now remember the dead*
>
> *who were once as you are now*
>
> *who are now as you will be*
> *in time*

### Circles

Standing on the edge
of the seat of the outdoor
toilet I looked down mesmerized
into the black void
reeling dizzily until
you made a rush to grab me
before I could fall.
You beat me in hysteric fear.

Crossing a mountain brook
on a narrow plank
I fell in and this time
Papa beat me in fear of heart
gingerly.

Standing on the edge of the deep
end of the Taxenbach swimming pool
I stared into the water until

all swam before my eyes
in concentric circles
pulling me in to complete the pattern.
I don't remember falling in,
only being pulled out by
my parents' friends whom
I was with, and whose pale
anxious faces greeted
my eyes on reviving.

Having nearly drowned went beyond
a beating: there was
a silence in the house that evening,
and a fretful sadness for me.

And at night the razor blades
slashing into my pupils
relentlessly,
a demon fantasy;
or me, on the borderline
of waking and sleeping,
growing instantly
vastly tiny,
shrinking more and more
in an infinite plenitude
of all-engulfing empty silent space.
Revolving concentric circles in my mind
and I was looking for the hole in space

to let myself fall through
and be saved.
from what?
to what?

### 6. Recitative

Now you are dead,
mother mine,
and have been in the ground
for many turning seasons.
I did not attend your funeral,
but stood at your grave
a month later
alone and bowed
listening to the late summer silence.

I am glad I missed the ceremony,
for I would have spoken bitter words
to wither the crow-priest's glib platitudes.
Thank god with death it all ends somehow.

Who'd be so foolish to
wish for the endless blight
of unadulterated immortality?
This immensity of greed
needs metaphysical short-circuiting.

I recall your face frozen
with the chill of hopeless
doomed age where nothing
can ever get better
this side of the grave.

The trees and leaves and snows
and flowers and clouds and birds
and the sun tell us of the seasons
of our lives,
and all that we can know.

The mind must dance a duet
with time,
else wither or shatter
in disconnection.
The felt rhythms count
for more than we can know.

With shame I remember my shame
at your sickness, my searing shame
at you, my mother,
my self-distancing and exile,
uprooted from the soil
of human-heartedness.

Solitude is the consolation
of an empty heart,
the throne of pride,
the atmosphere of sorrow,
the alchemy of insight.
Solitude, the curse and blessing
of self-consciousness,
I owe you good and bad;

I owe you words and thoughts,
which are a kind of action
and a kind of anguish.

When you died mother
I rejoiced for you
and was glad that
you were set free at last
from the unkindness that sets the tone
in the world.
Politicians, pimps and prostitutes
of all feather
flock together
and always manage to get on
at the expense of others,
but the few good simple honest
people everywhere
o my do they suffer.

No words can say it,
nor deeds undo.

You are free and unburdened now,
those who cling to the surface
of life like leeches
never shall be,
and in that too is a kind
of consolation:
greed always sets the tightest
traps for itself.

Bitter benediction, bitter words, too harsh, too many.
To begin and end in forgiveness is the spirit
of the word. But bitter words must be spoken,
without them no renewal is ever possible.
But to be bitter ever after
surely is a case fit for laughter.

      Look to the Rose

To forgive oneself
is to forget oneself
and open to others.
Look to the rose!

for Elsje

It was all gold
your hair
it was all shining
your body
it was all aglow
when the sun rose
and entered through our window
and when I entered you
it was all rose blossoming
it was all dawn.

Look to the rose!

the pointed fragile-sprouted blossom sides
fanning out to form a crown of glory,
sun-born in the rhythm that turns the tides

breaking on the weathered rocks, or rushing
on, out-spent at last in sand-ribbed rivulets,
unlike the late-summer rose, full-blushing,

brandished, rainbow-splendored,
but chiefly lovely red:
o in the beauty of the rose
is the heart of all
forgiveness and peace.

## 7. Benediction

The truth of asters and roses rests on your grave tonight, the
wind's in the trees,
the clear stars overhead,
forget-me-nots in the garden at home,
the sound of lake-waters by the road,
and peace in the heart.

Past and future are relative,
the present touches eternity everywhere
among the galaxies,
the mind must a dance
dance with time,
the body bloom

and hug its life
in an inspired breath.

Words my speak of this sometimes
on festive occasions,
but for the most part
the mystery of tuning in
to the turning years and seasons
and the constellations of head and heart
revolving forever fiery in space,
infinite in and out breathing
is hidden deep
in the wellsprings of the heart.

O look
    look to the rose
    to the glimmering morning star
    to the setting sun
    bathed in blood over the mountain's head
    or suspended silently above the sea

in peace of heart look at these
blessed scriptures of our human season,

time's flaming epitaph glossed
in smiling breathless wonder:

blessed are the living,
and blessed are the dead.

# Living In

living in a washing machine isn't easy.
i prefer the frontal type,
the ones with the spherical
plexiglass doors where
you're not quite so scrunched up
and dropped in.

you've got a view of the world
of sorts with nose and forehead
pressed against the foggy tinted
glass of the hatch
the gums oozing lint

tumbled and whirling about
sopping wet, suds draining
from eyes and ears and
the hair a stringy mess,
like spilled spaghetti.

as long as the setting isn't "white"
but "delicate" the living's manageable,
though one is jostled to a frazzle
and blind dizzy a good deal
of the time.
life, after all, is
an endless alternating cycle.

on sunday mornings it can
be quite idyllic there
curled up in a daydream
like some silly sailor
in his hammock,

or a soapbubble suspended
in the summer air until
some blasted fool of a
customer drops a quarter
down the slot and

the water comes splashing in
and dammit,
the bubble's burst again.

# The Wheatland Diner

I'm just finishing lunch in this diner
where I've eaten for the last three years
when it suddenly begins to move.
It lights out so damn fast that I spill
my coffee, and by the time I get the mess
cleaned off my lap, we're passing
the town limits. A crowd of people
cheers us on as we run a red light.
Pretty soon we're whooshing through
those wheatfields like a greased surf-
board and the farmers are so open-
mouthed their chewing tobacco
plunks right out. Now it's near
sunset and for Chrissake we're
shooting through Death Valley and
how in hell am I going to explain
all this to the wife and the boss?

# Thirteen Ways of Looking at a Teddybear

1. teddybears make the best of friends
because they never talk back and
just ooze sympathy

2. i called in sick
and said my teddybear
would give the lecture

3. he did,
refusing to participate
in the questionandanswersession
afterwards

4. cocktails have never
agreed with him

5. he seduced the neighbor's cat
who had an abortion
not wishing to bear
teddycats

6. his eyes glint
in the corners of the room
on moonlit nights

7. he sighs and searches for lint
in his paws when it snows
or i sneeze

8. he's allergic to ezra pound and jellybeans

9. if he refuses to go to
the potty i tell him i'll replace
him with a rocking horse
or a parakeet

10. he doesn't like to go to the zoo
because he's jealous of the
tiger's and the zebra's stripes

11. i harangue him when i've had
too much but he just sucks
on his cloth teeth and stares
into space in lotus position

12. he says he'll leave me if
i don't stop writing about him

13. the rest is silence

# Strange Noises

strange noises split my skull.
i'm at the bottom of a well.
the stars are very far away.

faces of people that i know
paper my walls grimace green,
mirrors leer antiphonal.

i count the pulse that doesn't count.
my arteries run riot, ravel,
and wherever i go
is where i'm not.

the red of the red of my blood
reels in antipathy
as the words parade on
with craven majesty:

is the moon false or true,
and what has the sun to say on its behalf?
saturn interrogates its rings again,
and wombats are all the rage this year
in outer mongolia.

must i nod my own agreement?
i demand it here and now,
for god's sake, say yes, say yes.

the mind frets the strings
of its experience
with shrill monotony,
i smash my aching head
against the unseen bars

that thud like pillows and muffle
the drum of my bruised self.
deep down my heart
the greedy bit takes, bites,
gouges, growls, howls its victory

and searches fathoms further
for some ultimate blowout strike.
words are vultures.

the red of the red of my red,
aghast, turns pale in protest,
boils, boils, and froths to frenzy.

i'm at the bottom of the unheard well,
the bucket's rusted out,
the stars are very far away.

my head's had one too many,
my best dreams have all declared
bankruptcy and gone
straight down to hell.

# On My Thirtieth Birthday

I sit and listen to the spaces
in which people come and go

the sound of a car coughing up
a bird startled into flight

a leaf falling in the void

a child crying out of nowhere

I live in the margins
between word and sound and motion

for in these suspended spaces

I'm silently at home.

# letchworth park

i awoke at dawn and heard the green
call of the wild wood sounding
in my blood

it was good that i answered
for there in the forest
motionless i heard all
the voices of the unseen
birds among the branching
trees interlacing my field
of attention with their never
ending joyful crying out

i felt once more the depth
of my life that i'd nearly lost
in the noisy prattle of my ever
so selfimportant days

returning home for breakfast
i even tasted what i ate
and saw the yolk so yellow
and egg sparkling white

# Planting

It's unromantic work this
putting of seeds in the ground.
The sun is behind my back,
climbing down the shoulders
of the rolling hills as it
showers us in red. My neighbor
hands me the packets,
tells unpracticed me how far
apart to space the seeds,
and my clay-crusted hands
hold I don't know what
green shoots to be.
The finger-digging is tricky
too, for there are fragments
of glass and rusted cans and
wire lacing the ground: feckless
tenants' remains who used the
garden as a dump. Such minor
hazards will repay us in long-
eveninged August with sweet
corn, huge squash gourds,
cukes, plump tomatoes, beans,
cauliflower whose moist lush
taste will linger in our
mouths through the mellow
Indian summer and October
with its fallow light at
sunset after the days are
shorter and work seems longer
and more wearying. My back-bent
garden task, though unidyllic,
seems just the right thing to
take in hand this late-May
evening when thought seems
out of place, and idling would
be nothing more than idleness.
It's good to touch the future
even in the shale soil of this
upstate farm whose poetry can
wait for more privileged moments
of sweet doing nothing.

My neighbor grins as he watches
me finish the last palm-full,
and hands me a hoe to smooth
over the shallow furrows. I
straighten my tired back and
watch the bay horse behind
the sagging fence watching me.
He too must be hoping for just
the right touch of rain to
quicken ground and blood.

# December 25, 1974

1

i sailed beyond the tonnage of my days
this fall striving to tell all:
about shakespeare, for instance,
about the romantic spirit, for instance,
about myself, even.

2

reaching for the place of knowing
beyond words.
now it feels so good
to be void.

3

the moccasined sky moves
with tufted feet of wonder,
but those lazy snowmuffs, the clouds,
waddle at their own crazy pace.

4

yesterday on the lift i watched
my dangling skitips bisecting the hill,
sailing above trees and skiers
and waiting to whoosh like hell.

5

in the plunging moment of snow
my childhood flared
as the poles marked off
the whistling turns.

6

awoke today to a brilliant snowfall.
now sudden gusts of wind shake the houses
and the trees that shed white wraps

7

and now again it's just the glistening
unmoving expanse of the valley
in its bridal of fine-spun drifted snow.

8

handel on the stereo and then the stones,
lemony light patches
flecking the clouds

9

the moment of the mind's pulse
and the december sun,
windswept beacon of the sky's shrouded horizon
watching for the new year

10

that janus season.

# New Year's Day Poem (1975)

loincloths wrapped around skeletons
stare with pointed eyes,
children's angular faces and empty bowls
implore our sleepless nights.

on the launching pad of our benevolent plans
justice fizzles out or topples down.
and in the economy of nature
it has always had
a very low priority.

sheer numbers engulf
our bloated apathy:
so many then, so many now,
and so many more in the next decade.

arm! arm! and steal a march on time
for it is very late.
what's to be done?
the margin of survival grows constantly slimmer
for those who flicker on our screen.

Dr. Kitter Witter my cat
disdainfully sniffs
the chewey t.v. wowee
Superkan Katfood
while the empty thirdworld bowls,
grown gigantic, scream
through hall after hall
of abandoned hope
and shattered innocence.

what's to be done? and what's to be done?
the chorus of troubled conscience
is by now a mere void of repetition.

the thought police will know
lurking in the sinister recess
of some dark political alley
to waylay and rough us all up
in the coming years

the thought police
the uniformed but uninformed
the wasted world, the ciphered ones
in rigid hateful ranks,
yes, the thought police will know
in international networks of
unending demotic gray.

and in a quieter, subtler place
further along that unpaved way
on the twentyfirst station of the cross
inlaid with razor blades
and etched with human blood
some vast supercomputer whirs
its spidery circuits
bleeps a million lights

and boots up with a wonderful
metalectric appetite

to munch us all for breakfast.

# In King's College Library (Cambridge, June 1975)

Here behind an ancient cloistered window
again after seven years
surrounded by eons of ideas
pressed in books that live
in the mind
I look out at a green
expanse of sun-splayed
manicured lawn and the
ageless spires of King's
Chapel and drink once
more at the well of peace
I am so sorely
in need of.

They say all the cells of
the body are renewed in a
seven-year span: so I'm
a new man, yet the core
of the old lives here in
my heart and in the gothic
stones of King's and in
the time-polished escritoire
at which I dream and
in the very grass.

This place is so much in
my heart and ever fresh
to me: slow turns about
the Fellows' garden,
the stained-glass oratory
of the Chapel, the spiced
ritual of the Hall and
the arched rhythms of
the mind sustained here
in King's library on a
clear sunshine morning.

It's good to be back,
I said to myself when
I saw the spires of
King's two days ago:
this June-bright day I
know I've never been away.

# Purest Form

i live on the circumference now,
refining the forms of my nonbeing.
below huge floes of ice drift
in the dark waters.

there's a column twelve thousand
feet high. at the very peak
i perch and survey
the divine emptiness
all around.

what a relief from plenitude.
what a relief!

the air is cool.
at night there's the glitter
of the starred firmament,
then the flamingo dawn flares,
then the sun dips into darkness,
spilling itself across the sky.

this is my rhythm now.
living pure, or pure living
on the circumference of
my atmosphere, far above
where the blood tides heave,
the agony of mud, the lucre
of inane doings, the pangs
of ingrown greed, the perpetual
blather of fools.

i live on the circumference now,
serenely poised atop
my crystal perch

waiting for some vast leap

when my parachutes will blossom
with silent marvel
at the utter emptiness
that redeems the shrieking
plenitude of teeming
raucous life.

nothingness is purest form.

# The Sleep of Genius

is long as a frog's moment of terror
before the snake's icy gaze
and hot darting tongue.

long as a mummy's yawn
behind the granite slabs
of a museum that winds for
thirty subterranean city blocks
in daar el salaam.

long as a dinosaur's pinched ribs
beneath thirty tons of shale
in what was once a pharaoh's garden
and now is an abandoned rollerderby
rink that you drove thirty miles
on a sleety road to find
on a lonely saturday night
in kansas for a blind date
that never showed somehow.

long as the journey of a dime through an age of ultimate quiet.

long as a *llano estacada*
without sun or wind
when all the clocks have stopped
and your dying breath won't
tremble a single candle's
flame and sand slowly
fills your gasping mouth.

long as a hangover
after three weeks of hard
drinking when they are drilling
the pavement for new pipes
under your south philly
bedroom window.

long as the hangman's frayed noose.

long as a silk curtain's rustle
three miles down the waxed corridors
of versailles palace at midnight
in marie antoinette's bedroom that you
alone the locked-in-for-the-weekend tourist
can just hear as you pray for dawn
with your hair
standing on end.

long as a cat's nap
in the outer fringes
of the crab nebula

long as the knowing smirk
of the mona lisa
two days from now or
sixteen centuries ago
long as her salacious lashes
or the landscape decomposing
behind her shawl.

so long

is the sleep of genius

that
    i can't
        really
            even
                begin
                    to

# Saturday Morning

I'm waiting to play basketball
at ten. It is now nine
and I've filled my ball
with fresh air (carefully
having squeezed out the old
which didn't give a proper
bounce any more).

I will meditate for fifteen
minutes, concentrating
on the baskets in my head
so that my outside shots
will go swishing through.

Shortly before going down
to the court I will run
in place, jump and touch
the ceiling a few times
for good luck, do knee-bends,
loosen up my arms, and think
of positioning for
the rebounds that are always
just beyond my mind's reach.

Then I will sit perfectly still
again for a few minutes
savoring the dancing moments
ahead that I've been waiting for
all week behind the workdays' inane
clamor of mere busy-ness.

At the age of thirty-two
I am just learning
how to play.

# Journeying

*"Nel mezzo del cammin di nostra vita"*

1

At the age of thirty-three
I feel that I am half-
way through my life.

This could be a mistake,
of course, because I may
only live to forty-eight,
or alternatively—who knows—
get to be a hundred and two.

On thing is constant, though.
I am still waiting for things
to fall into place,
for some sort of pattern
of meaning to jell

or even (one learns to
be satisfied with less)
for a hint or pointer
to emerge in barest
outline, to whisper
with half-bated breath
the intimation of some
fundamental indwelling
significance.

Significance?

I know this sounds
vague and foolish,
but it's what I've
always thirsted for
as far back as memory
will take me.

2

As a child I was chock-
full of wonder in a world

of unmanageable possibilities.
Anything could happen,
and sometimes did.

The sun changed its place
in the sky between naps;
a friend was hurled across
the road by a motorcycle
that roared out of
nowhere. Furled in a
flag of blood, he was
whisked by a fire
engine to a hospital
where he later gave an
audience to his dumbfounded
friends, bragging of
multiple injuries.

The doctor had the only
private car in town; its
lush red leather upholstery
smelled like roses and like
old ladies' gloves. It made
clouds of dust as it rattled
down the road; it also made
a noise like incessant
farting. One lordly day
I even got up the nerve to
ask for a ride, which
was granted. I had to
walk for miles through
the dust just to get
back home, smelling
like roses and like
old ladies' gloves.

Anything:

In the springtime the hillside
became a gurgling network of
secret underground water conduits
that we reworked into a system
of elaborate dams and sluices.
One night the moon disappeared
altogether in a perfectly

*A Little Fire in a Wild Field*

clear sky. And the village
priest got drunk and fell into
the sewage tank that workmen
had opened up. He emerged
to general laughter, reeling
ripe. And for no good reason
a sister got married to an
American G.I. and was spirited
off to Philadelphia via
Graz and Italy, waving from
the window of an express
train with the gestures
of another world. *Auf
wiedersehen.* Fare thee well.

And do they wear the same
clothes in Philadelphia and
go to school and church?
Do they play soccer
and ski in the winter?
And does the sun shine
there the same as here?

The first time I visited
her in the States one of
the first things I saw
after baseball and Howard
Johnson's ice cream was
a big shiny black bug late
one hot summer night that
seemed to move more furiously
than the Roadrunner in the
cartoons. It was my first
vision of the cockroach, which
introduced new cataclysms into
the world of my dreams. No
insect should be allowed
to move *that* fast.

3

In school I didn't understand
many things the teachers tried
to drill into our heads,
like electricity:

I could use it, like
everybody else, by
flicking a switch,
but where was its
secret? The teachers and
the books could explain
up to a point how it
worked, and why it got
from here to there in
a line, but nobody
ever said a word about
what it really was.
I figured everybody
knew but me, and that
I didn't because I
was just plain dumb.

I still don't know,
though it took for me
to become an adult to
catch on that others
don't know either,
really, even those whom
I still look up to as
honest-a-god magicians,
those lucky ones who
can fix a t.v. in a jiffy
or make a conked out car
run again as smooth as butter.

There were so many things
of which teachers and
parents and even friends
knew the how, but not
the what. I was chiefly
baffled by the latter,
and still am at thirty-
three. Goddammit anyway,
what's the what of what,
and why and wherefore
are we?

And in school I never believed
the catechism answers because
they seemed so silly. Why

*A Little Fire in a Wild Field*

didn't Christ have any
girlfriends? Why did our
priest drink beer and play
cards at the Gasthaus on summer
Sunday afternoons? How come
God threw Adam and Eve out
of Paradise after they exercised
their free will to his displeasure?
How was it possible for the body
to be resurrected after thousands
of years of rotting in the ground
and be reunited with the soul?
Wasn't that a little much to
ask of anybody to believe,
even children? What did
people do in Heaven except
pray and go to church forever?
If the Devil existed, how come
nobody I knew had ever seen
him, not even Otto, the village
idiot? How come my father
never went to church and groaned
when my grandmother gave her last
Schillings at Sunday collection?
How come God let his only son
be nailed up on a wooden cross
by a bunch of beef-brained
Roman soldiers? Why did people
have to suffer? die? be born?
Why did my grandmother scoff
at the town's few Protestants
as *the new heathens*?

4

I was sure that all those
pressing what's and why's
that I couldn't get to the
bottom of as a child would appear
as clear as sunlight to my
mind's eye once I'd be a
grownup. So I waited for
that day of truth to dawn
somewhere on the hazy horizon
of the future. Even in my early

twenties I still believed a
fundamental pattern of meaning
would jell within a given
number of years. Sounds
fatuous, doesn't it?

Well, I'm still waiting for
things to add up, and for
the penny to drop, as they say,
but with a good deal of raw
perplexity now. Deep down
I've come to fear there's
no end in sight to my questioning,
that nothing ever will come
clear and plain as to those
what's and why's, even
the shape of my foolish life.

5

But then in another mood
I know full well that if
things suddenly did come
together in a fixed network
of final meanings, life
could only become
as dull as hell.

To define is to confine,
and at best we want to live
in a world of untrammeled
possibilities. It's the boundless
we go journeying after,
for less than all cannot
satisfy us thirsty pilgrims
of the dusty road.

The center of my life,
I realize now, has always
been a peekaboo game of half-
hidden meanings. To sound
to the bottom of those
ultimate why's and what's
for which some ache and on
occasion even die would

untune the strings of
the mind's experience
and short-circuit the
performance in which we
all have a part to play
so long as we remain alive.

It isn't easy to remain alive.

As I approach the half-
way point of my trek
through time I begin
to see that the last
thing I hope I'll ever
be able to find is
the secret of what or why
that I've been hunting for
in my own haphazard and
dilatory way all these
years. Any mystery that
could be simply known—and
god forbid—put into language
(no matter how subtle) would
trivialize the monstrous,
ecstatic burden of our
endless journeying, would
revolt Job anew and return
Lear anew to the boards with
a magnificent barrage of
protestation; yes, would
dumbfound even Faust's
impervious striving for
the unattainable and make
that Spanish Don give up
his blessed foolishness.

6

So as I travel on
toward the second
half of my days here
under the sun that shines
on all of us in some measure
I'm full glad to know
that whatever goal consciousness

may signify is as undefined,
boundless, wonder-full as
the paths of the stars through
the billennial skies of time
and space, and that we are all
of us single points of light (and
some focused as intense as laser
beams) signaling to the unknown
within and without through a
glittering universe awash
with vast tides of
omnivorous darkness.

And anyway, if you think
about it, thirty-two isn't
such a bad age to be trekking
wide awake without a pocket
map or compass pointing
to fixed goals.

I'll just feel my way
a step at a time as
I go journeying on
to where and what
no one can say.

Maybe I'm even more
choked up with wonder
about it today than
when I was just a boy
aching for replies
to my relentless
what's and why's.

# Turnpike

My skin hums at eighty
miles an hour.
Tires sing and twang
on the warm concrete.
My sweaty palms have grown
into the steering wheel.
A fat bug splatters
on the windshield.
I pull out and pass
a huge truck crawling
up the grade.
O shit! At the top
of the hill a patrol
car lurks in the grass
divider. I hit the brakes
before I shoot by him
and swallow a heartbeat
or two. I see in the rear-
view mirror that he's still
stationary on the grass.
Close call! Down goes the
accelerator, my eyes
are reeling off the road,
my shoulders hunched.
I'm whipping along past
eighty again as I feel
the pavement in my fingers.
I'm triggerhappy on
the turnpike, running
a quiet race with myself
hour after hour. Any
minute now a thunder-
shower is going to burst.

# At Home

They squat in front of the tube
in the livingroom and slurp
canned beer by the gallon.

Outside it's 99% humid,
in the kitchen the icebox
purrs. The baby has wet
itself again but will have
to wait until the next
commercial.

There are more riots in South
Africa and hijackers are running
amok everywhere. Undisturbed
by the evening news
grandma sits on the Sears
sofa and knits a coffin
out of violet silk.
It is supposed to rain
again tomorrow.

# Day's Done

These late summer evenings
the haze rises off the land
so heavy you can almost seize
it with your hands. The fields
are veiled and gauzed,
mist shrouds trees and
rows of corn, and the sun's
a yellow-reddish suffusion
above the raw horizon,
waiting to drop down.

At night the sheets are
soaked with the sweat
of my free-floating fear
that no fans can blow away.

Day's done again and
the jittery wait for
dawn mines the no-man's-land
of my self with unstable
deposits of nitroglycerin
and I freeze to a scarecrow
for hours on end.

# Marriage: Point Blank

Two mummies sit in the mausoleum
of their livingroom and tear
the winding cloth clean off
each other's bones.

Furniture invested with eons of feeling
gone stale looms colossal.
He thinks of plunging into canyons.

She says she hopes there's a god
who can see her hidden suffering:

He thinks, for god's sake, let's
leave god out of this.
The carcass of the past
malingers on the carpet.
Are these stains congealed blood
or pus or lymph? And who's
going to make it come clean?

She weeps tears bitter as gall
and chokes on the fishbone
of Married Bliss.

Tons of silence press down
on his neck as he dives at
the bottom of a black hole
without a single ray of light,
unable to surface or send
a cipher to redeem his life.

The years hang in the balance,
the scraps of their posthumous union,
the husks of unlived experience
and the overdigested emotions
that ulcerate their very guts.

Shall they make a clean breast of it
or a hash of leftovers
and serve it at a mummy feast?
She's pickled rosebuds in a mason jar
and kept them on a cellar shelf.
And he his Sunday feelings
in the unfinished closet.

Neither dares blink or show
a hint of pity. Into love's
crocodile eye they stare

    point blank.

Reader, say a prayer for them:
these who once loved
can now feel only

    the pain.

# Diotima to Socrates

So Socrates the dialectician
desires to be instructed in the wisdom
of love by Diotima of Mantineia.
Dialectics, Socrates, is an art
that freezes up the blood, but
I am a midwife who helps deliver
the beautiful soul's progeny.

Well, then, Socrates, listen well and learn:
love binds together men and gods, love
goes between, love lives in the breath of
poets, sages, priests; love, my friend, is
the source of the true spiritual beside
which all other arts are merely vulgar.
Nature and man are forever laboring
to give birth, o Socrates—procreation's
always current—but the true poetry of
the soul is the longing to be delivered
of the beautiful, a diviner begetting
than merely doing the bidding of the flesh,
though that too can participate the divine.

Even vulgar arts like money-making,
rhetoric, gymnastics can be based
on a genuine desire for the good
and the beautiful, but the usual
course of these is to get side-tracked
into mere vanity and self-preening.
Love, in other words, is a thing of degrees,
each of which is readily pervertible.
The glorious moment of the flesh's flame when
the beautiful in the male and the female
meet in finest balance and are wholly
consumed in one another's arms, this pitch
of the body's and of nature's highest
flight is easily reduced to mere
lust for flesh, and from there, further debased
into a slavish and most gross greed
for things, the husks and dregs of what was once divine. So much
for the corruption of the body's
natural flame, that drugs and goads the world,

but that in its purer, nobler forms can
make up the lesser dreams of true poets, lovers.

All love, Socrates, craves immortality,
but the higher forms proceed only from
pregnant souls, which birth conceptions
of wisdom and virtue. These are mysteries
accessible even to you, my friend,
but there are yet higher, hidden ones which
I cannot say if you will ever reach,
or if you can mount aright the gradients
of love. The way here is to begin with
the cult of all beautiful forms, then
to focus on a single one and to create
from it fair thoughts in your mind, to fathom
there the innate measure and mold of all,
which breaks the passions' slavery to that
one, and opens out our higher being to
the love of the indwelling form in all.
Now you are ready to perceive the naked
splendor of the mind that dwarfs mere outward
show, that animates any noble law,
science, art; all measures of the mind that
move like music, dance like the stars to the rhythm
of the whole. Purged of all narrow vistas
of the petty self, you now intuit a
vast universe of harmony, you move to
the threshold of a single science of
beauty everywhere, the kingdom of the soul.

Thus love leads you toward the true end, which
is the sudden sight of an unchanging,
primordial order of beauty: there nothing
waxes or wanes, grows or decays, but remains
perdurable, intense, refulgent, pure
like the completest crystal, ruby, pearl
washed in an eternal wave of the sun's light.
This, my dear Socrates, is the secret
pinnacle of beauty, supreme, simple, tensed
high above the mortal clouds and the dross
of the foolish, the base, the greedy, the vain,
the prattling herds who rush in their giddy rounds
to gull one another in the swamps and
deserts far, far below, where only
the natural sun scalds their narrow skulls

and all pledge cheap anthems to the bloated
goddess of mediocrity triumphant.
But always a few simple, fated souls
feel the force of that beautiful form
in their minds, and love draws them on and up the
long, laborious path that leads to that
eternal pinnacle which, if achieved,
consummates in perfect cosmic union
the seeds of joy and beauty dwelling in
the individual soul. Yet of the few
who travel that narrow, treacherous path,
o Socrates, only now and then one
pushes on through to the peak, in spite
of all danger, privation, unspeakable despair;
and in that single soul's moment of triumph
when it touches the top after monumental
trials of endless effort and aspiration,
man becomes god, and the divine fulfills itself.
This, Socrates, is the perfect pitch of
love that all desire craves, however
blind or impure, for the godly substance
within strives forever to complete, to
express itself without, and although nearly
all who aspire to perfection needs
must fall short before the demands of the
distant goal, those who reach the peak in some strange
fashion do redeem the rest of us who don't.
The only truly base are those who never
strive, content to slumber in the mud,
for mortal man, my dear Socrates, can
become a friend of god and be immortal,
after a fashion, by mounting upwards
in the scale of love, which is also truth,
wisdom, virtue, justice, beauty, more things
all than may be said with words, even between
the wise.

Hush, now, Socrates, and do not
question with your clever tongue, but look
within yourself for the glimmer of the truth
that is forever beyond the reach of
any dialectic.

# Ravings of a Mad Dog Poet

I have been as crazy as a mudturtle in a monsoon
yet thought dazzling thoughts that could wrench
the continents into new drifts.

I have been as ungracious as a mad dog to good friends,
I have been as polite as a trained seal
to the people I despise the most.

I have raged and cursed the fallow dawn,
chewing my pillow to a cud.
I have also heard the voices of divinity
in the first shaft of dawn's
breaking light.

The Great Wall of China is but an inch
in the longitude of my dreams
but I don't have the courage of even one
and dare less in a decade than I dream
in the journeys of a momentous night.

I have hated myself, loved
myself, looked up, looked down,
looked right through
my simple self.
There in my most secret soul
I have even learned to fear myself,
which is perhaps the most important.

I've been a strong hater all my days
giving heart and soul to it.
Don't show me people who can't hate
because they ain't.
Those who turn the other cheek too long
will end up permanently kissing
their own ass.

My diffidence is only matched by my pride.
Sometimes I'd like to kill all the people
who spout the slogans of the day,
and sometimes I'd just like to kill myself.

Sometimes I'm plug-ugly and scare
the crow on the tattered fence,
and sometimes Robert Redford's just
a malignant turbaned Hollywood turkey

next to me.
I have been as strong in my ignorance and vanity
as a skunk.

I am so full of self-contradictions that my soul is at least
a thousand and one.

I wouldn't want to give up a single one
even though I see most people don't
have the honesty of facing up to even
a paltry begging morsel of one.

I can go from one to a thousand and one
and all the way back
in a split second

and never even blink.

# Help

A young skater has broken
through the ice toward the middle
of the pond. As she
keeps trying to pull herself
out of the water, the firm
ice keeps breaking off under
her numbed, grasping hands.

How cold she must be what with
windchill factor and the failing
light of the late
winter afternoon.

Desperately she calls and calls
for help as she keeps
grabbing for more ice
to save her.

Someone toss her a rope!
throw her a ladder!

But whatever you do
for god's sake don't
try and walk over and
haul her out
because as you draw
close the ice will surely
give and the two of you
will touch in the choppy
waters of your meeting

only to drown.

# Somewhere

Somewhere deep in the hold
of the luxury liner there is a
hole no bigger than
an egg where the water
pours in incessantly.

The Captain can't be held
accountable, but the hole
is there nevertheless.
The liner is so vast
it could take thousands
of years for it to sink
with all its passengers
and crew swarming up
on the decks.

But the second waits,
with eagle eyes it keeps
a sharp lookout for
the moment of disaster.

Where is the hole?
Where is the Captain?
He who could sound to
the bottom of this affair
would be a life-saver
for sure.

Somewhere deep in the hold…

# After the Concert

I'm the man who folds all
the chairs after the summer
evening concerts
on the lawn.

If the heavens are webbed
with black I don't
touch where owls or
bats perch
but move
from row to row
like a somnambulist,
harvesting crumpled
programs, a grumpy bar
of Brahms, ringing
Wagner leitmotifs ditched
behind a concrete post,
a few Strauss notes still
cavorting among the rose
creepers, a half-empty
beer can on the lawn.

After the furthest voices
have faded in the distant
parking lot, the gallery
of switched off stage
lights pings out traces
of heat as it restores
the equilibrium of the
spent evening.

Great white-winged moths,
fried half to ecstasy by
the brilliant fire of the
stars, twitch numbly
on the gravel.

As the bulging ship
of the moon sails through
staggered canyons
of clouds I count
ticket stubs and
watch the dumb death
dance of the moths.

# A Little Fire in a Wild Field

The vast fires of the stars are stoked
in billion year cycles, but I will try
what a small fire in a wild field yields.

My master unbuttons in a naughty
night to swim in. Wild geese do not fly
that way, where men contend with stars and rage.

And I for sorrow sung that great fires
burn unchecked, anneal, destroy the day
to the bone. Little fires fuel the mind.

A dog must to kennel in the rain, but
I will start a little fire in a wild field.
Great wheels crash down the hill; the fool will stay.

*From*

# Paralogues

*(ca. 1977–1979)*
*there are monologues*
*and there are dialogues*
*but these are mostly*
*paralogues*

# Dorothy to William at Alfoxden

Well, there I was at the breakfast
table clearing away the dishes when
my brother William called out

"Dorothy, it is the first mild day of March;
Each minute sweeter than before,
The redbreast sings from the tall larch
That stands beside our door.

My sister! ('tis a wish of mine)
Now that our morning meal is done,
Make haste, your morning task resign;
Come forth and feel the sun.

Edward will come with you;—and, pray,
Put on with speed your woodland dress;
And bring no book: for this one day
We'll give to idleness."

He always was the sweetest rhymer,
that darling poet brother of mine.
Anyway, my woodland dress was in
a laundry tub, and little Edward
was sulking because I'd caught
him in the pantry with his fingers
in the raspberry preserve, and I
had to play taps on his hindquarters
to remind him not to forget himself
like that again. So he wasn't at
all in the mood for taking in the
first sweet minutes of March just
then. And as for me, well, William
had dictated a whole sheaf of lyrical
ballads the day before—expostulations
and replies, and tables turned, and
anecdotes for fathers, and lots of
lines written in early spring—and
I still had to copy them after break-
fast and the dishes.

I'm always Dorothy, his little sister,
secretary and housekeeper. I do keep
a journal, though. Be that as it may,
I still had all this lyrical copying
to catch up on, so I just called back,
"Dearest William, you go on ahead and
feel the sun; enjoy the blessed
power that rolls about, below, above;
I'm too busy just now making clean
copy of your spontaneous overflows
from yesterday. So run along, dear
brother, and drink the spirit of the
season, while I trim a new goose-
quill and set to work."

# Demon

the demon stalks,
i shut my eyes,
the image stays.

long hair trails
the afternoon,
black, blond, red, brown

strands exacerbate
the mind's pulse
to fevered pitch.

what have i done
*this* to deserve?
why do all other

forms dematerialize
before such pure
sufferance of

iridescent beauty:
rise and fall of
breasts, sway of

thigh, curve of
back, for god's sake,
even turn of

ankle! why this
burden, weave, burn
of speechless craving,

wordless wonder
so dumb-struck
with demon forms

that never stay
the mind's pause,
stanch the flame?

# Hungry Eyes

the hungry eye bleeds the world
thirsting for the forms
it contains.
desperado cockroach skittering
across the surface of a ground
always in retreat,
vampire prince in exile
seeking to render all
that elusive latency
a radiant presence
in the pulsing
here and now.

Voyeur prism, all-
hungry globes to swallow
the globe, incorporate
the banded flesh,

your unstilled longing
for form upon form
deconstructs, scatters
the self, bonds its
movement to a further
movement:

craven eros
where harbors
your home?

what place can sustain
what vehicle contain
your frozen motility?

what irrefrangible flight
loft you to some still point
to anneal your
hypertrophied need?

as eyes bleed
only the silence speaks

# Television

Pellucid center of the world you claim
to scan, cool bright eye, clear lens of a stage
you set as much as mirror, what bold train
of thought could undo the myth of the age
you have mastered with such a subtle spell?
So crude and crass, so very quiet and well
reticulated with fiction the sheer fact
that your bought retina projects life forms
you lie to reflect in an unseen pact
between the viewers and the viewed. So norms
of a seeing we have made ourselves are
taken for the iron rules of some fate
apart from us; and scope, range, limit, bar
of what we're made to see, we see as innate.

# Heidegger's *die Sprache spricht*

as if we were in need!
no record needs the day
of how it was spent
when the voice finds
itself, no calendars
of before or after.

*die Sprache spricht:*

creatures of difference,
bread and wine born
between earth and sun,
tolling that silence:

words speak.

as if we were in need
of more or less
when the word bears
the bread and wine,
still syntax of
the living air.

as if we were in need
when voices vowel
the day, as if we
were in need when
need itself
finds a voice.

# Syllables

billboards syllable the night,
elongate its silence.
a crack widens as it is crossed.
the hand of a friend
clenches to a fist.
the noise behind the screen
of noises jells to a massive
statue that governs the
annealed foreground.

the ringing of a bell
slides ten years back,
fifteen, across the hard
surface of time,
and everything is
and is not
the same.

the stones of buildings
or brooks burden the
moment because their
epic vocables cannot
be voiced by any tongue.
the mouth can't shape
their substance into human
forms, nor the mind
bear their bulk

although teeth flash
in different rooms
behind caviar and
crackers as the void
syllables drool down
the sides of cocktail
glasses in bejeweled,
ringed hands that cast
skewed shadows into the
spaces between all the
words that have ever
been vocalized.

# Burial Grounds

there surely are too many teeth,
and libraries the graveyards
of teeth. some ivory even on
those polished shelves,
so that the boards bend
beneath their gathered
mass seeking to sink
back into the earth
and become like those
elephant burial grounds
in India that we read
about as children.
and then somewhere in
the thousand-year future
some exotic ivory-hunter-
museum-curator will come
with a vast paraphernalia
and dig up all that hidden
wealth and stuff it into
lucid cases with learned
labels as ladders to a
forbidden past,
moving his teeth,

moving his teeth.

# Blackout (NYC, July 14, 1977)

when the light
failing to gather
decenters itself

the dark is on the make:
into buildings,
down subways,
through our mouths
and eyes.

denuded parking lots
lour, advertising signs
shroud the evening in
mute embarrassment.

bereft of the cover
of light the true
shapes of the city
spring into action:

the violator fuels his
torch, shows his erection
to the secretary cowering
behind her tinted curls:
she only senses
what's *there* for her.

the professor is blind
before his text in the tomb
of the auditorium,
and his mike, like
the priest's, announcer's,
geek's won't cut
the silence.

the avenues and back
alleys have a life of
their own as the police
and the policed confound
themselves under the bright
arcs of floodlights
rushed to location
without any script.

the shape of city is
the crouched beast of
the dark which the fled
light would tremble
to deliver.

# Don Jose

Don Jose rides the level
sands on his stoic
dromedary, not looking
before or after.
what would be the point,
after all, of such
vantages. the sun,
a giant squid, hugs
the horizon for
which he heads. he
meets a woman by a
tent whose waveblack
hair shrouds the sands.
she cries, "I burn! I
burn!" so she burns,
he thinks, she'll always
burn. so much for her,
he reflects to the
placid rhythm of his
desert horse as he
keeps crossing to the
line of the horizon.
one by one his tracks
melt in the sand as
that odd woman moans
through the tent of
her hair as if it could
make a difference.

# Shadow

Shadow came,
Shadow said,
"man o man
you dead."

I gulped, goggle-eyed,
and turned my head away.

Shadow came,
Shadow soughed,
"I am the voice
of the far-down
earth, arteries of
coal and diamond,
oil-charged aortas
under desert dunes,
muscles of mineral,
volcanic bowel
rumblings; my granite
nerves measure the
globe where no
sweating miner's
lamp has ever
probed, no rig's
bit; fire-tongues
of the liquid core
below the cooling
tides, streams,
lakes, I am.

My throat holloes
far, swags your
neutral trim with
lava bursts,

I am the Shadow man
of rock bottom,
tonsured with wide
rivers of scorching
light, hear my
heart's sheer clarion
or feel the desert
sun strip the flesh
from your bones,
faltering headman you,
more fool than fool."

Goggle-eyed I gulped
like a flounder on
parched ground and
turned—o grief to
say—my gills aside.

# Souls of Light

I have seen, been, done,
felt many things over
the years, but last night
lying in your arms for
the third time that day
every movement was the
thing itself, every touch
a final coming home:

O Elsje Elsje lying in
your arms such tenderness
I never knew there was.

What two souls of light
could do through all that
dark was within easy
reach of quiet hands,

and did we ever sail so
smooth under a milkmoon
sky on that shoreless sea
spellbound through the night.

# Cross Country

> *"Inmitten des Seienden im Ganzen west eine offene Stelle. Eine Lichtung ist. Sie ist, vom Seienden her gedacht, seiender als das Seiende."* –Heidegger

So quiet blazing white a day I have not seen.

When one pushes the heels firmly
down the wax particles on the ski
surface lock onto the snow crystals
firm enough to make a sort of
launching pad for the skis

the manual explained.

After our halting beginners'
efforts we achieve an extended
push and glide rhythm,
loping with cinematic ease
through acres of white.

Our thoughts too get a sort
of purchase on this land,
grip steady enough to push
off and move swift,
silent, clear.

To and through the woods,
and then a wind-
swept clearing.

A German philosopher said
that poetry too is a kind
of clearing (his name an
omelet of heather and eggs),
Teutonic sage rapt with
abstractions that accumulate
like snow.

You drift in your full-down
parka over the snowfield
like a blue swan on a frothing
tide, azure Elsje luminous
above the endless white.

You glide back home,
I push on into the orange
feathered dusk.

Shotgun reports of far-
off hunters I never
see go: pop, pop, pop.

Two dogs stationary in
a field I pole into,
one brindled, one big
black with spiked
collar and sparkling
teeth, make my heart
take a turn. As they
begin to lumber along
a row of trees at the
border of the field,
suddenly some large
brown game bird explodes
skyward out of the branches
as the dogs and I stop
dead in our tracks:
flip flop, flip flop
goes my heart.

Dogs and bird are gone
and in the aftersilence
the grip of my hands on
the ski poles eases as
the image of a belly-
speared hound slips
out of my mind.

Under the sickled skylamp and
the first diamond stars high
up, before the full rush of
dark, I stand in a pale wash
of light at the top of a
hill in an eerie clearing,
eying the shadows of the snow-
draped bushes, the far-away
village lights sprinkled
against a crimson horizon,

glittering necklace
of the coming night.

I gather my thoughts to shoot
down the hill on target for
the bull's eye of a trail
opening into the woods. Twice
I take a wild spill because
I can't make out the mouth
of the tunnel as I speed
closer, tumbling over and
over in a delicious failure
of nerve. The third time,
right on course, I plunge
into the dark heart of the
wood effortlessly as occasional
branch-tips whip the top of
my head. Once there, I
let myself fall on my
back, having achieved
the day.

On the way back to the farm
looming large now in the waning
light I stop and watch a burst of
wind sweep a thin current of
granulated snow with tremendous
velocity over patches of
perfectly polished lustrous ice
(proud salvers of the winter air)
and gust wildly up the valley's
tree and bush-dotted slope
wrenching from its mastered
irregular shapes noises no
words could hope to match,
material syllables of the
frozen ground blasted sky-
ward with stunning force,

bullied voices of the wood,
throat-wails, ice horns, stone
reggae, bitter stubble whistlings,
fluted wind zingers, sheer
ice shrieks, earth words

as odd and old as
these my thoughts.

things    thoughts    sounds    words

merge and settle for a second
on the screen of consciousness

      and then go poof

like the fir-topping of fine
powder snow exploded by the
bushy touch of a doe's tail
bounding by underneath,
and the flying moment of snow
settles down and jells
into a quiet blazing white.

These fields, slopes and woods
we crossed today in full winter
will never yield our tracks
even to the moist heat of mid-
July, nor our lives their
crystal instants beyond
reckoning, forever formed
and found anew.

So full and white a day I have not been.

# Paralogue

After working your way
down ill-lit corridors
that make the Pentagon seem
a cinch, you've come at last
to an off-white rectangular

room, unfurnished, windowless,
no pictures, chairs, no door save
the one you just blundered through.

White light so bright it blinds
your eyes suddenly floods the room.

To turn back now would seem
beside the point: the very
thought of retracing your steps
gives you the creeps. No place
to go, and you know that you can't
hang out in this empty space
forever. So where to now,
you clever young spelunker?

Why has the cat got your tongue
just as that pool of white light
drains inch by inch through the floor?

# Dream Log 1

A group of people in a decorous *salon*, familiar yet strangers. A large bluegreenyelllowbrown globe in a corner. Eddying currents of afterdinner conversation. A very selfassured boy—strong, handsome, about ten or twelve—is telling me with much energy, enthusiasm, and a wealth of detail, about the geographic features of the different continents. I, who have always been absurdly ignorant in geography, listen, impressed, delighted, amazed, and inquire: "did you learn all that in school?" "No," he exclaims contemptuously, as if school were a haven for the stupid. "Are you kidding?" interjects a refined looking *grande dame*, who I didn't know had been eavesdropping, "he learns all that strictly on his own, they don't teach them *anything* in school." True, true, there's no denying that school today is pitched at the lowest common denominator, and never at the gifted, I reflect. And suddenly I feel much concern for this clever, precocious child, for his inquisitive intelligence, his bright learnedness, and I am thinking of a diplomatic, non-condescending way of warning him that much intelligence will bring him much suffering as a grownup; to rein in his brains by all means before it is too late and the harm is done—at least to keep his knowledge to himself, because the ordinary detest nothing as much as learning. Just as I am ready to speak, people rush to the window because there is some sort of commotion outside. Curious, I make my way there too, and see on the street below a motley troupe of entertainers making friendly, ritual gestures of greeting and invitation to some sort of show. Suddenly I get it: the circus is in town! The advance party bows, they do tricks, there are bright reds, yellows, blues, the whites of clowns' faces, balloons floating to the sky. I am particularly amused by a redvested trick rider prancing on his trained Lippizaner whose hooves keep sliding on the slippery pavement, yet who always manages to maintain his precarious balance. At the end of this little performance the troupe bows, and in departing deposits presents on the sidewalk, including a fancy and expensivelooking bottle of liqueur which everybody in the room seems to have their eyes on, just waiting for the act to leave so they can rush down and be the lucky one to carry off the prize. Just then a wonderfully tall circus giraffe and a bulky elephant appear on the street. The giraffe bends down its endless neck, and with great verve, picks up the bottle and straightens out its neck again—its head is now at the level of our secondfloor window! The elephant is visibly jealous; he wants the bottle too; he lumbers over to the giraffe; his vast trunk stretches all the way to the giraffe's distant mouth and nimbly snatches the bottle out of it, clutching it with a tremendous elephantine smirk. What huge grey greed! I'm at once delighted and nonplussed, and wake to the noise of my own silly laughter, a bright wash of colors still jangling in my head, sounds jingling in my ears. And—strange to say—yawning lazily and rubbing my eyes, I feel as fresh and as bright as the dawn.

# Dream Log 2

The bluegreen lake at Zell am See, emerald
in the setting of my senses, childhood's
undimmed jewel. But on the narrow shore bold

housing starts sunder water from the woods
climbing sheer up the mountain slopes. I shudder
to see the wide scar of a road winding toward

bare summits lost in haze. I climb on up
past what was once all wild, shun a boat shop,
a service station a mile later, tap

my head in disbelief as a bold claque
of trailbikes goes stuttering by, speechless
I am, far past grief or hope. Turning back

I see David Caspar Friedrich forest
kings stretch their green gothic limbs right up to
the sky. My eyes travel up trunks that attest

huge force. Sudden I am lifted, hurtled
higher than trees, mountain peaks, clouds, mist,
to a sheer skyblue expanse of light. Startled,

I find myself gazing down at a glass
box, a sort of crystal display case
at whose center rests an open book I face

with wide open eyes, spelled way beyond (what
I ever was, am, might be) by big, bold-
face type, black marks on white. Strange script

fixed beyond the dance of life
invites me: so clear, crisp and bright
those simple letters printed on the page.

# Perhaps

Have you ever sensed the light
ice crystals of empty silent
space course through the stream
of your blood for an incalculable
duration between one heartbeat
and the next? Have you ever
heard the firm tent of the firmament
tear and shred, and glimpsed what
is beyond to appall your glib
mouth? The sky unseamed and no
way to word to void interstices
across which the mind forever
shuttles? Have you ever in a
frozen splitsecond of nonbeing
sensed that the sound of a needle
dropping into a glass of water
in Afghanistan would set you
off on a triumphant pilgrimage?
Perhaps you're ready then
to get to a beginning.
Perhaps you even can.

# Paraline

I am riding the line of the horizon now
close behind my shadow which I chase
and flee. The fleet-hooved stallion
knows that shifting line, and keeps us
right on target, moving as it moves.
If I can keep us on this line
I need not look before or after
but gallop wind-free with the velocity
of dreams. No idle noises now,
only the scrinch of rocks at noon,
the taut reins hissing in the wake
of the sun, the flashing hooves
playing out the centered line
through earth, water, air and fire.
The stables never asked us when
we left what we meant to do
nor where we thought to go.

# November Moon in Bloomington

Like a blank frozen syllable
you lurk in the sky
too remote from me
and unapproachable through
any ladder of thought.

Paleyellow Novembermoon,
shrouded Turnersun, so unconscionably
other, more sunk into yourself
than Northland Friedrich could
ever unfold with visionary
dreaminess of color, brute

midwestern moon, so unsayably different
from what we ever are,
unendingly thin cipher
your blank syllables shatter
the vessel of my spirit
into tenthousand arctic smithereens
and there's not the prayer of
a word that could merge them again

you skysail so full of silver so far
up there, incalculable point, so
charged yet void that I could bite
my tongue to pieces to speak

you, wretched moon, frigid old
vagabond of the long winternights
that move through the soul like
unending freighttrains of the dark,

you inhuman sliver, you unknowable
you which makes me shiver.

# Never Quite

She found her way to many
men's arms but none of them
ever found her. She forgot
that she had failed the history
of tenderness, so that all
these moments were the rehearsals
of unfeeling, the void *frisson*
that never quite…what?
True, she felt, but these
feelings were never quite
*the* feeling, so that always
in the after she knew herself
somehow betrayed like all those
times before. She didn't burst
into any new seas, and her
many lovers found no green
continents of joy but gasped
like drydocked sharks in
the nets of their numbed
senses. Her fingers played
no such songs of flesh as
could balance a star,
and what hands touched her
keys only brought forth a
dwindling repertoire of off-
key tunes. And every spring
such a bright rush of
flowers and blue light
to pain her wide-open
eyes and appall her
hungry heart.

# Miraculous Escape

Why did the rotund husband
as he came home drunk one
night to the big stone house
on the Chemin des Poiriers
overlooking Champagne sur Seine
enter by way of the cellar stairs?
And why did he fall right down
a deep well smack in the center
of the basement that wasn't
there the day before and that
was never again seen after
that night? And why was he
able to make such a tremendous
ruckus so far down the wellshaft
as to wake all the sleepers
in that huge house so that
they all rushed right down
to the cellar and managed
somehow to extract him from
the mysterious well in which
he was so solidly sandwiched?
And why didn't he have even
a scratch on him as he emerged
clamoring at a great rate about
the outrage and indignity of
falling down a sudden well in
his own house in the middle of
the night? And how did such
tragedy averted turn into a farce?

Surely the answers to these questions
are as important as to any
that could be asked.

# Luther's Blues

*(for Luther Allison at the Bluebird,
Bloomington, Indiana, December 8, 1978)*

Blue haze, red ceiling lamps, a float
of raised faces on a sea of shadows,
scent of booze, grass, flesh. Swatches
of talk turn to glad whoops, moans, whistles,
yells as Luther and his band launch
off into their set. How the frantic bursts
and shrieks of the elongated notes ease my
deepdown ache, ill will so rampant that I
can't begin to utter it. Luther plays that raucous
electric bluesguitar like it's a part of his own
body. Wailing bloodbeat, soulwoe overflow
the dayworld barriers that keep us all apart.
The pulse of time becomes a space in which
audience and band are one, where sound is as
material as a pitcher of water, a piece of
driftwood, these swaying breasts of a denim-
shirted teendancer. I feel it in the blood now
that music makes good will as Luther wildly
works the wailing strings like a lover
disclosing perfected passion. The ecstatic
touch that banishes before and after is upon
us with its mastery and we are sung beyond
ourselves to a place that opens only after
years of deepdown devotion to the demands
of an art where that which is distinctively
human can emerge spontaneously, as if
by accident, for the first time here and
now, and always when true music
sounds the soul.

# Young Heine Calls on Old Goethe in Weimar

When still green in years, a mere
stripling of Apollo's art, cheer-
ful and bold I footed it to
Weimar in Saxony, through
an August countryside, to gaze
on Goethe reign above the haze
of summer in Olympian calm.
The dusty banks offered balm
in the shape of juicy plums
which I relished. Many suns
in the firmament of literary
fame had paled before my contrary
gaze, but this god dazzled me to a dot,
for Goethe shone above the lot
of lesser fry who claw and scratch,
connive, intrigue, and hatch
plots on the lower slopes of Parnassus
like bugs stuck in thick molasses.
His outward figure matched the form
of his mind; calm, to greatness born
the clear gaze of his eagle eye;
in accord with earth and sky
his firm and noble bearing, unmarred
by low humility, the reward
of worm-like Christian piety
which with a surplus of sobriety
clogs our cheerless latter day.
But before I go astray
and preach or whine, let me
get back to Goethe: so free
his face, and yet his stature grew
when he spoke, and when to you
he'd stretch out his hand it was
as if his index could give laws
of motion to the pathless stars,
and his smile stop Titans' wars.
Supreme like Jupiter, father
of gods, he stood, why bother
to tell you of his eagle and

the bunch of lightning in his hand?
I thought to address him in Greek,
but before my simple and weak
phrases could be turned I guessed
that he spoke German. The rest
was youthful folly: in my awe
I could hardly move my jaw
but stammered that the plums I ate
between Jena and Weimar were first-rate.
Many a long drear winter night
I'd dreamed under the moonlight
about the sublime, profound
and clever things I'd say to astound
the famed sage when I'd meet him.
And when finally my fond whim
came true I could only bleat
that the Saxon plums taste sweet!
But Goethe smiled. He smiled
with the very same lips that beguiled
Europa, Semele, the Danae, not to mention
ordinary nymphs who caught his passing attention.
Goethe died March 22 of last year.
*Les dieux s'en vont*: only Europe's kings are still
                                                                            here.

*from*

# Alcatraz of Hope

*(ca. 1980-1981)*

# Strand of Hair

Once in the back of an old classroom
I saw how a single strand
on a full head of black hair
canceled out a lifelong dream
as if it had never been.
I sat in my chair
in great despair
and watched my world
founder on a thread
as thin as air.
That was years ago.
I've traveled everywhere
through a world of hair
but still in my mind I'm
frozen to that chair
like he who made man
was chained to his rock.
You might say a single
thread gave me a lifelong
shock. And though my heart
beats and I do what I can
to shuffle through my days
a single black hair
will never let me be.
Though friends give me a hand
I no longer know who I am,
nor where.

# Lazarus

When the words of that strange
preaching man called him back
from his untroubled sleep
the sudden light blinded
his eyes as he staggered from
the grave, trailing bands of
white linen between his wilted
hands. Pale like his shroud,
he wished for the silence of
the ground betrayed by the voice
that exposed him to crude day.
But then his squinting eyes
fell upon a Magdalene standing
by the bearded Judean's side,
and again he saw the thick
locks of black hair snake
down past the full curve
of the thigh, felt the shape
of breasts, savored a whiff
of honey or senna. As his
dead rod rose to the pulse
of desire he was almost
reconciled to his new-found
breath. And he pitied
the speaker who had the power
to recover others' lives yet
knew nothing of this in
his own. And Lazarus walked
right past Christ
in bliss.

# Foundering

We build up an habitual hebetude,
clothe ourselves from naked life
for whole decades on end until some
odd alarm of first spring, a sudden
quirk, a soundless blow sledge-
hammers us to smithereens:

the fleeting touch of a hand,
for instance, or the way a pink
tongue will suck across a row
of teeth, or the brute
locking of thighs.

The hurt of being thus fractured
is a birth pang, as if
we need to be broken down
to grow again,
manured by pain and joy.

Ever so sudden today I was
sped in a yellow butterfly van
across a velvet plain

then sang in a Pacific of
anemone hair like a school
of ecstatic dolphins

then fisted the thick white
mists of the sky as a sceptered
thing of the clouds

and then again sat on my worn
sofa in this too dull and proper
room and in the mirror watched

a tear wash my cheek,
flotsam bead of my foundering

on this monster reef
which breaks and breaks
and makes me whole.

# Night Noise

All through the night we can hear
the huge roar and whine
of straining engines, and
in the lulls the backup
beepers of construction trucks.
Even when we reach to touch
we can't ignore it.
Great floodlights chase
the dark and watch the dirt
churn under colossal blades
and claws. In the early
morning monster metal insects
with ribbed rubber wheels half
as big as a house go clattering
down the dirt road that runs
by our place. They are finishing
a highway less than two miles
from what used to be our quiet
retreat in the country. On the
evening news we watch long gas
lines in Washington, Pittsburgh,
Buffalo, Boston, New York, although
the stuff is now a dollar a gallon
and rising fast. The energy
crisis pinches believer and
scoffer alike, but at the
center of this road-building
ruckus there's no crisis of
will nor failure of nerve.
That sound and fury will slice
with brute precision between
farmland tilth and village drowse.

It knows no doubt, it's sure
of what it's about, and we
whose night rest is sorely tried
deplore as much as we admire
its intransigence. Just as
the gas runs short the Interstate
snakes to completion. Not even
the planners ever claimed it would

bear much traffic, but it had
to be built. "To be defeated in
our victories doesn't make
much sense," whispers the voice
of my intelligence. But our cats
are not fazed, nor the bumblebees
by the chestnut tree, nor the rats
in the rotting barns.
They disdain to let on
about what we don't know.

# Trite Mykonos

Whitewashed windmill against thatch
of brightblue sky, freak pet pelican
in a sidewalk cafe, chalkwhite winding
alleys, stuccodry sound of cicadas
in the olive trees, crowded bus to a
quiet beach, fat lazy lunches followed
by wine naps, waves crashing against
the rocks of a postcard harbor in
the evening breeze, coastline under
the blazing belt of the Milky Way:

twelve student summers ago
I spent a few days on Mykonos;
off and on I've fantasized about
living a whole year on an outoftheway
island in the Cyclades in a little
beige cottage watching the sun
slide up and down the azure
Aegean, writing some unoriginal
poetry, rereading a few good
books, eating and sleeping
simply and well.

Someday maybe I will go: get
the year off, save enough to
see it through. Someday, sure,
but in the meantime these ordinary
tourist snaps will have to do.

Trite, hell yes, but true.

# Dialect of Unknowing

Perhaps I can stay to hear
the edge of buildings. And
taste those brave asphodel
salads when they cavort
at the elephants' ball.

I cannot permit the numbed grief
of my senses to hasten my
leavetaking. They shall yet
know themselves for what they
are, and bow to each other's
wakened selves with mandarin aplomb.

I will wait for the full sail
of my words to steer star zones.

I must gird myself for my absence.

Then is when the prom of my perplexity
is sprinkled with green carnations
on question-mark tuxedos.

My pocketwatch ticks me on
as overdue, yet the gala
invitations to the performance
of my splayed vowels and consonants
keep flooding in.

I will toy with these until
I know better because
I know no better.

The whatnot grass, the crass bluejays,
the stumbling yellowjackets of late
October, my candy-striped pajama top
astride a redandwhite director's chair
harass me with their persistent
certainties. Still I shall
postpone being's dossier.

I must dither with all these things
until I can sound them in a dialect
of my remotest unknowing.

With the false modesty of middle
age I must eat of that tart
tree that mumbles that no
better can be had.

I want to wait so as to be able
to simply say: this is where
the chips fall. No asking
*why*, only grasp the *there*.

I no longer hanker to construe
the sentence of my being.
The faint trace of a few
things on a few words
will do to plot the axis
of my bewilderment.

# White Wood

From the cozy hearth at the center
of the farmhouse I can hear
countless ice crystals flurried by
the whitemooned winternight
plead with a zillion teensy voices:
*come to the dark heart
of the February wood
and be like us.*

Only I can hear these minuscule
diamond choruses trill above
the hum of the shifting winds
and slanting drifts. Across
the blanched fields
they sing to me.

And I must leave the lure of
my woodfire and go in the bare
strength of my bitter need to
sit an unsculpted statue
in the blind snow,

to hold my blank vigil
beyond any profession until
the first light of dawn
flecks the new horizon,

to squat in terminal silence
through the concert of the cold
until an expiring breath
congeals my lips,

I an ice crystal among ice crystals
in that unbroached singularity
of benighted snow.

And dark even at
winternoon is that dark
heart of the white wood.

# The Wall

1

The motherwall only delivers us
to another which never gives.

2

It had been there as long
as he had been.
He thought:
what if one could
fall down from it,
Humpty-Dumpty-like?
But he never could conceive
of the possibility of
positioning himself.

3

To cram the void self
had been his plan
all along but there
was the wall which
could not be broached.
Nor would tangents help,
and ladders there were
none high enough.

4

The lines in his hands
began to match its
fissures; print of
palm and stone grew
so close it was hard
to tell them apart.
It was only when
the wall became his
touch that he nearly
forgot that the wall
persisted in his cells.

5

Often he wanted to run
upon the wall like a
Roman upon his sword
but the wall was
everywhere.

6

Always between absence
and presence, granite
of wall, unmitigable,
his unstinting need
circumvented by the
unalterable other.
His thought came to
assume the outline of
that uniform limit,
languaged it as a
structure of what
was lacking: wordwall.

7

He penetrated women
only to touch the rough
surface of the wall.

8

He knew if he could posit
the wall as the condition
of his freedom (rock
boundary that disavows
all east and west,
past or future)
then…what?

9

He dreamed he could dance
with himself in pure
presence beyond any
parenting, loss or

begetting, but there
was the wall, now
the line of the horizon,
now the concrete an
inch from his nose,
now his stone-palm:
his Alcatraz of hope.

10

The invisible wall
became his need so well
that in his perennial
running up against it
he found his lack
substantiated, his
need affirmed by that
limit to his will.

11

He thought it might
yet be possible to
define himself through
his negation, to
trust himself to
the absolute difference,
to jog the long mile
of his stone self.

12

He thought and thought
the wall.

# Gorgon

Snake eyes, you have turned
my eyes to stone.
One of you would have
been enough for what
the three of you have
done for me. Poisoned
looks, and then some.
I'm frozen now for keeps.
The hand can't find
the sword to settle
your score. The pen
is jammed between
my fingers above
a page as blank
as any arctic waste.
Snake eyes, you who
came unasked to my
annulment, you who
have chilled my
very teeth,
eschewing any curse
this only return
to you I make.

# Needle's Eye

After the inane agonies
of the millennial cranium
I have now learned to profess
nothing. Unmaking of myself,
chastened by those inevitable
finitudes. And so many passing
moments I had mapped as
a crossing to the remotest
stars. Now I must not
even dream of them.
So far they are behind
me now in the illusory
profound of my most
private space. To hold
to the present is not
to cipher, to be as
empty as any wind, to
not let others teach
you what you no longer
care to know, to
confess yourself
a derelict of aspiration's
endless etceteras.
Profess it now,
the huge vacancy
of the needle's eye
after the needle is
no longer there.

# Plastic Surgeon

Nature gave you one face
but I make you another.
I remove a rib, mold and
trim it like a bow, insert
it to straighten your misshapen
skull. Delicately I push the sponge
of your brain aside as I operate
around the optic nerve without
blinding you, reposition your
eye-sockets to allow an
unobtrusive gaze to fall
upon an altered world. My
hand delves in your dark
and bloody mouth, my scalpel
moves with the precision of
instinct and experience honed
for years; my gleaming pliers
crack your upper jaw which I
let float free in your soft
membrane and then reposition
and anchor in new flesh
moorings; I stitch up
the lining of your mouth
without ever beholding what
it is my aching fingers do.

Today I cut, crack, saw,
chisel, peel, slice, scrape
and mold to recover the first
innocence of a face that never
was but as the map of your hidden
hopes. My only plastic is
the transfer of the gleam in
my eye to the remodeled planes
and lines of your facial bone,
tissue, skin; my only design
is to make your gross visage
over into the form of love
you carry within and now
suffer the torture of having
stamped on your outer shell.

All this I labor to deliver
knowing the great hurt I cause
is to sculpt where your cruel
genes betrayed you with such
crude and casual abandon
toward your true and shining self.

My only craft is to unfreak you.

# Triumphs of Paranoia

Twenty-four hours a day
the invisible cuckoo clock
ticks just for you. Only you
can hear it, or see the trillion
connecting fibers that make
your brain the central
switching station of the globe.

By your whispered wish
gold prices drop precipitously
in all the money markets of
the world, the Russians steal
a march on Kabul, an ayatollah
tyrannizes a country, or a French
philosopher cashes in his
existential chips. And henceforth
doughnuts shall have no
holes in the middle.

Although you number mighty
enemies among the power
brokers of East and West
you are certain even in
the agony of your persecution,
like Christ crucified,
of the final vindication
of your supreme mission.

Next to you hydrogen bombs
are mere matchsticks.
Your faith in your own
omnipotence has gone beyond
anything; you can afford to
smile benignly upon the foolish
doubters you have honored with
token confidences of your
grand designs: the skies will
remain blue for now: so much
you have intimated to them.

You take a certain comfort
in the knowledge that you
rule by silent fiat an age
in which even Presidents'
wishes are minutely foiled.

As the last straw of your
megalomania you have granted
yourself the consummate wish
that your empire shall never
know any bounds.
Supreme you sit at the center
of your universe, disdaining
in your self-assurance to
destroy all those poor
wretches too obtuse and
obdurate to acknowledge
your omnipotence. And all
earth's insects sing
only your praises.

# Pet Phobia

Every dwelling you move into
seems already occupied by them.
They are the world's most prolific
breeders but shy to put in an
appearance in broad daylight.
They prefer to announce their
presence in the crossing from
dark to bright. Behind bathroom
and kitchen baseboards they lurk;
at will they roam the deep night
until the sudden flick of a switch
shoots them like errant bullets
across floors, sinks, countertops
and walls for cover. You've also
seen them late on hot summer
evenings whizzing over city
sidewalks with the self-assurance
of infernal messengers. And you
have become well-schooled in
their different sorts, from little
brown to big black, having watched
them indoors and out with the mounting
fascination of horror in places as
diverse as Philadelphia, Grand Bahama
Island, Bloomington, New Haven, Crete.
You have collected lore from obliging
friends, one of whom, a zoologist,
told you of palm-sized ones in the Amazon
Basin and of a species in Madagascar
that can hiss. And your discovery
that the long brown outdoor ones
can even fly gave you a new insight
into the apocalyptic possibilities
of getting the creeps.

With eyes agog you have learned
to stare at the blur of their legs
and brittle carapaces as they scurry
and whir from the light. They have
splintered the quiet of your dreams
as you have crunched them underfoot

by the scores in vain. You know in
the ageless folds of your brain
that they have been since the beginning,
that they will preside as honored
guests at some black parody of
the last judgment, that only
their evil feelers will quiver
when the rest of the universe
is frozen into stony fear.

To appease the dark powers you
have finally adopted the cockroach
as your pet phobia, yet you
sincerely doubt the olive
efficacy of such an offering.

So whenever you so much as
catch a glimpse of one
the frame of your world
cracks and you swoon.

# Litany of an Expiring Mouse

The bright dribbles of my red
are already congealing on
the evening porch where in
tomorrow's heat black flies
will buzz and wanton.

Two huge fur fists slam me
down whenever I try to
focus my blurred resistance
to make a dash for the lawn.

Two eyes like close green moons
giggle, fangs close on my heaving
sides as I jerk and wriggle through
my last gasps. My velvet skin,

silk flesh are deep-furrowed by
feline claws, my final sense is
searing pain pitched against hope-
less whiskered odds. Teeth will

do the oldest work when my dry
eyes sponge up the moist night
and giant jaws scissor off my
hinder parts. Only my marbled

guts will greet the fluted dawn
as the trophy of my playful
hunter's careful snack. In
the pedestrian agony of

a torture enacted through
eternities my cuddly purring
killer and I affirm the first
blood bond of a nature

back to which you who have beheld
all this in rapt and stunned
attention really do not
want to get.

# Hands

Each day the old man's sinewed
hands push the boat against
the tide, but the tide always
pushes it back against his
calloused palms. Although
the boat is never launched
the struggle is daily renewed
where land and water meet.
His friends, long since pensioned
off, shake their heads and
take their ease by their
peat fires in their seaside
cottages. They have grown
weary of even watching the tide,
the ancient's hands baffling
the sea and the seasons;
theirs are folded lazily
over contented paunches.
They think them wise.
But the aged veteran of
the tide's mighty leap
and swell is lean and strong
as a board that bends but
never breaks. He knows
he cannot lose as long
as the tide has not won
from him his will. His
heart brings hope to
a hopeless task, his
salt-sprent shoulders
and arms loom large
against that inevitable
surge as his spread hands
forever front the elements.

# Winternight Dream

*(January 1981)*

It has to be winter,
not soft-gurgling spring,
nor full-blown summer, nor
autumn bursting and wan,
but a harsh winter so
chill that you spit ice
into the ferocious air.

In the cold clasp of cruel
February you will savor an
austere solitude far from
the glad yelps of perennial
summer's tourist pack,
frivolous notes of
a slight interlude.

In some out-of-the-way spot
where no trails lead to your
rough cabin deep recessed
in the Adirondacks you hazard
an odd blend of soul-vigil
and hibernation.

Here you will have to shoot
or trap what you eat, or
live off what stores you
managed to carry with you.
The woodburning stove on
which you cook also keeps
you warm as the Northern

storms rage about your
hideaway. You've even had
to cut and split the logs
which save you from the bitter
cold. There are no other
guests save the elements
and you in arctic communion:

unless you count a few
classic books: glittering
works of the mind clarified
by time in the night of
our blood. These and

yourself you will scan in
the far-off woods like
the blazing print of
the Northern constellations
before dawn when silence
fills the air like snow

cold comfort of a season
when you know that only
self-teaching has any
lasting value and that
in such a monastery
of the mind more learning
may be had than in our
landscaped universities
with all their mummy lingos

that can never glow like a
wood fire or a singular
movement of thought in
the dim Northern night
when the chaste winds blow
the snow foot-high about
a cabin in which you sit
stoking the flames' slow burn.

# Unbidden Guest

A pheasant came to us to dinner,
though unasked. Hurled by
a huge gust of wind,
he crashed against the front
of the house with a great
shock, like a shotgun blast.
Broken-necked he lay
with his graceful head
askew, his fiery plumage
drooping by the frozen
shrubbery. And instantly
a red carnation bloomed
beside his shattered
mouth: blood on snow
screamed so bright
my senses reeled. His
limp body still warm, I
carried him to the wood
block where I split fire-
wood and chopped off his
head. Elsje bled and gutted
him in the kitchen sink,
then baked him slowly
in the oven. His lean and
gamey flesh was garnished
with an improvised sauce.
What this midwinter storm
brought and our hands
prepared sat in our soothed
Sunday stomachs leavened
with a dash of guilt. Why
should we not take unabashed
what the season gave unasked?
Never had we hoped for this
yet our eager mouths drooled
at the feast like any predator's.

# The Sky's the Limit

O I wish that I wished I were
riding through the Tyrolean orange groves
in a pristine Philippine submarine
jostling those humdrum pippin days,

that the amber Aztec moon wore penny
loafers and cracked the cinnamon pavements
with silver dragons flashing bloodphosphorescent teeth,

that vast and vapid feline gods would spit out
the maudlin world like a huge psychedelic
furball and schnorr themselves to infinitely
multiple orgasms,

that hilariously hyperactive future museums
in Moscow, Rome, Washington, Peking and Paris
would celebrate for millennia plus the high
mass of our collected follies for the gaudy
boardwalk adoration of a credulous past
worshiping with party hats and hyperborean bloomers
our cuckoo images on sandalwood mosaics silkscreened
across flamingo triple helixes of liquid onyx,

that the white haze of all possible cumulus clouds
would gather itself up into a humongous
tropical avalanche to stifle our madcap
filibustering pomegranate heresies,

and I wish that our wishes were like
a million Bedouin rice puddings with blue
whirlybird wings against a mauve sky
veering and sheering in all directions at once,
singing with huge camel beaks full of
Saharine silence, hump-swamped with light

and I a merest flibbertigibbet dot rising
against that sand-dune horizon
flinging and singing myself

like a rice camel forever on the equatorial wing
into that pledgeless and insurgent sky.

# Gnostic Song

O Manda, Manda d'Hayye,
sealed in my senses five,
noise-numbed by the shrill
world, aweary I am of that
bleak Tibil and the endless
traveling through
the bitter eons.

A son of song and light
I am, O Manda, thrown into
this black hole, this
labyrinth of fear where
the gross dance of
the generations holds
me down.

Far have I sunk into the well
of space and time, cruel
Rutha keeps me from
the shining sky, spark upon
spark of my bright being
dispersed into the dark.

The strange world falls
through me, Manda, and
Kushta knows me not:
I am aweary of that barren
Tibil. Hurled from
the axle of light
I seek to pass the Suf
Sea, I seek to regather
my far-scattered bundle.

A mere captive I am,
cast into foul sleep,
almost drunk with my exile,

yet my mouth still is full
of light, my head full of
air, and my heart,

O Manda, Manda d'Hayye,
my heart is forever set
upon the stars.

# Changes

Bitter changes are coming.
The house you seek to buy
will turn into a maggot
hive. Your friends will
go thousands of miles out
of their way to avoid
seeing you. The quick-
silver ponds will freeze
in July this year.
The lapdog next door
will howl until your
blood boils and you
shoot his master in
the head to find some
relief. New right para-
military units in green
will run wifeswapping
maneuvers in your neigh-
borhood. Your students
will begin to instruct
you about how dreams
operate when cost
accounting is at stake.
Various jellicose mosquitoes
will suck all the juice
out of your stereo.
The brackish lagoon of
your hopes will harbor
weird lunar alligators
with lapidary jaws,
and the hawsers of the
runagate ship of your heart
can only find moorings
on the orange quicksands
of your purloined fantasies.
Thalidomide babies with
homicidal octopus limbs
will sprout among the
tomato plants in the garden
you never sought
to cultivate.

# Professor of Desire

Desire doesn't fail,
only we do.
We lead stinted lives,
stifle wishes as true
to steer by as some
north star of the soul.
We betray our best.

And what for?
Small praise
great asses bray.
We renounce from fear.
We shake in our shirts
and compromise only
to hear ourselves applauded
as wise at last.
Only *we* are lost.

Wishes plead a truth
we ignore at our
cost. And that what's
past faces you on
the perilous way.

It makes no deals
with the you
you've never been.
It quakes, jolts,
pulls you until
only your shadow's
left to accuse a
heap of tatters
you've displayed
in false pride
with lying eyes.

No corrupt politician's
cribbed patter
can see you through,
no Dirty Tricks,
no silken purse.

That extreme passage
you will have to hazard,
your shadow sifted
to accuse a you
sorted to a pip.

Professor of Desire sez:
"pride of patience
is a scarecrow,
pride of prurience
fool's gold.
Strangled wishes
make no hay:
there ain't no use
to getting old
if you haven't
lived today."

# Weed Thoughts

Thistle-like weeds who have
begun to sprout and bristle
in astonishing numbers on
my untended lawn,
I gouge rootward around
your prickly spears with
a long-bladed tool
wishing I were a better
surgeon as I make brash
gashes and unsightly
earth-marks which I
assume will heal just
like any flesh wound or
even quicker. Unlike a
physician I wonder
whether my cutting is
to cure or only serves
my human wilfulness.
As I dump you in a
weedpile I have some
doubts whether in the
economy of nature I who
do the weeding count for
more than you the weeded
though I can't honestly
say that such thoughts
give me so much as a
moment's pause. Why
then I think them
I do not know.

# Lukewarm

It's that sort of lukewarm day
when the leaden sun makes no
promises save such as you
entertain through wishful
shills you refuse to credit
when they gloze on the threshold
of desire in some back room of
the wax museum of your mind.
That sort of day you know
so well you hardly notice
it. Such suns melt no wax
nor can the luxurious touch
of an ungloved hand break
the hard rock of your
unquarried heart. All this
you know until knowing
goes numb, like a hand
calloused with too much
handling, its shake a
lax snake refusing to
coil in a skin
old as death.

# Torn Ligament

Like the air you take
your body for granted
until something goes
awry. Invisibly it does
its job; you only notice
it through the absence
of its powers, or arrested
processes. This once meek
ankle now breaks your
stride—ouch!—this
broken string now turns
your song into a groan.
Now you need a third leg,
you hobble with a cane
like some arthritic horse
sent to haul a giant
load up an interminable
hill. Gravity, once your
kindly dancing master,
now pushes the spiked
ground against your
stumbling foot. You are
preoccupied by missteps,
by stairs, by how to
lie in bed, stand in
the shower, by how
long this thing you
never cared to know will
keep on harassing you.

# Hour Test

Under the lifeless spell
of neon tubes twenty-seven
students are hunched over
bluebooks, sweating answers
to my test. Such power
I have never learned
to relish. I can almost
feel their thoughts skitter
through the stifled air.
Later I will do my grader's
job, my head sunk down like
theirs are now, hands on
sweaty temples. Here I can
observe them with neutral
sympathy, sensing that
answers that can be lipped
or penned do not address
real questions. Take for
instance Virginia Woolf:
why doesn't that busybody
Mrs. Ramsey ever make it
to the (overly symbolic) light-
house with her oedipal little son?
that's a question I daren't quite
pose to these adolescence
ripe. God knows that nobody
ever gets anywhere, though
we're always on the move,
feet, wishes, or pencils
flying to reach or cross
some finish line.—Thus
I mull my useless thoughts
as the neon-oppressed class
strains toward the short-
term insights of an hourly.
The invisible vulture,
Hope, squats above the academic
sweatshop clock on the wall,
its vile beak sunk
in my puzzled brain.

# Man's Best Friend

will pee, barf, chew
on your Persian rug

dig holes or leave huge
turds on the front lawn

begin to howl just as you
are falling asleep

drag half the back yard
up and down your house
the day before the dinner party

jump on your back just when
you and your lover are heading
for mutual orgasm

growl and bare his teeth
at your guests, then
minutely sniff their genitals

keep you from ever going on vacation

and generally run amok
when you least expect it.

if any of your relatives
did such things you'd be
ready to sign on the dotted
line to have them put
away for keeps.

instead you pat him on
the head and call him
a good boy.

# Waylaid

Afternoon sunlight through study window

                                          fills room

wind billows white transparent

                                          plum blossom print curtain

toward me

                                          waylaid by

the fullness of being

                                          mouth full of plumlight

unable to speak or write

                                          silent I sit

# Centering

The bars of a bare and simple melody
rightly heard can become the echo of
the song of songs, make palpable
for the first time the note of the
beginning, before the empty hiss of
space was, or that fatal tick of
time. The work of art dwells in
the before-the-start. The first
outward speeding ray in the dark
chasm of an undifferentiated
universe is refracted through
the prism of the mind, broken
down only to be forced by
reflection into its proper
plenitude. The beginning's
indiscriminate profusion of
explosive energy is still sorting
itself out in the allotropic
mines of consciousness to get
some purchase on itself. And we,
yes, we—who and whatever we may
yet turn out to be—can, with
the printing house of the mind,
limn the traces of that first
setting forth with all the works
of man. As mere matter plunges
outward with nothing but entropic
momentum, the mind's gravity
seeks the center with all
deliberate calm.

# Hope

*(Once Again)*

The man who dares to hope brings
balm to bitter wounds.

The man who persists in hope
prolongs the agony of fools
and children's laughter.

He saves the future from itself
by salvaging shipwrecked dreams.

With bare hands he builds dikes
against despair, knowing
that is all there ever is.

The man who holds on to hope
is a lifer who refuses
the easy break to stay
for the full term of his
sentence, who will sing
stripes as he breaks hard
rock in a humid field.

The man of hope fills
the void center of a zero
with miracles of his own
making; always he's lured
by the bait of his own heart
beyond the moment's
bleak finalities.

The man whose hands seize hope
is pushing a great rock up
the hill of his horizon to
a place he cannot see but
nevertheless believes is there.

The man who hopes will place
high bets where he does not know
the stakes or game he's playing in.

Only the man who hopes earns his fate
even when seeking to alter it.

*From*

# Moving to the Country

*(ca. 1982-1985)*

# Moving to the Country

You moved to the country to put down roots,
to drag refractory cattails from the pond's
mucky bottom, to dig prickly thistles like a
fiend, to plant a few seeds in the garden in
late spring, to stain your fingers deep purple
and strain your back and scratch your hands raw
reaching for blackberries by the bucketful in
mid-July, to jounce your lazy middleaged innards
on a Sears riding mower, to sit through the red
red September sunsets sipping upstate sherry on
your redwood deck, to attend to nothing but early
morning birdsounds the whole summer through, to
find and lose yourself in a precarious balancing
act, to cancel the racket of the world by not
answering the telephone's shrill, to merely
vegetate, to plumb the weathered strength of
fieldstones, to cast off the burdens of others'
days, to think your own thoughts, eat your own
lettuce, tomatoes, cukes, and melons, to stack
or stain or saw wood, to build a fire in the wood
stove on the coldest wintermorning, to be snow
bound in December, windswept in February, sun
burned in June, to be as barren and rigid as
the November earth, to dream like the clouds,
grumble like the autumn winds, to be as numb and
dumb as the high noon lizard basking in the August
sun, to be as green as the midsummer corn, to hang
high in the air and then plunge like the hunting
hawk, to move with and through the seasons
and yet never move at all.

# Winter Hunt

Because they leave no prints
in the snow and because none
have ever been sighted there,
hunting elephants in winter
in upstate New York takes
consummate concentration
and an unbending will.
There are no long-barreled
big-game guns for sale in any
of the local sporting goods
stores, no carriers or guides
to be had for hire at any price.
The full-bearded natives with
the gun-racks on the rusted-
out pickup trucks are as
uncommunicative as the trees
and as surly as the frost-
bitten coyotes scouring
the abandoned state parks.
The deer season ended weeks ago;
the landscape's void of any
purpose save for your lone
search. The tall tales of
the gray mammoth beasts with
those huge trunks and gleaming
tusks go back to long before
the Indians whose descendants
still retell them over sixpacks
on their reservations. You
know they're there; your
spirit-eye sees a massive herd
loitering at the border of a
birch wood at orange dusk scooping
up the phosphorescent snow with
triumphant trunks. You will
track their lumbering canvas
hides through insensate winter
days and nights until they fade
into the torrential downpours
of early spring. Your only
token of success will be an

April mouthful of acid rain,
a misted-over, silver-barreled
elephant gun without a single
notch, and that itch in your
trigger finger for the passing
of another fall.

# Home

Home is what and where you trust.

The moment when you don't
have to prove yourself
but can approve of
even your mistakes.

Home is the place where
your face is the moon's
face, where the water
you sample turns into
the wine of your hopes,
where the line of the horizon
hums to the vibrato of
your dreams. It's the un-
choreographed ballet where
your furthest past and
future selves dance a
loving *pas de deux*, where
you and your shadow meet
to the alleluias
of your blood.

Home is when your lions
and lambs, eagles and snakes,
lie down to mate for your
greater good, and where,
beyond any mere calculus
of others or otherness
you are simply true.

# Bare

After I forced myself out of the warm bed at the first
fallow light of dawn and tramped through the damp chill
June fields down the hill to the rockhard brookbed to
watch the sun rise from behind the hill's horizon, and
after I trudged back up the path to the dirt road leading
to the farm

    I saw

    the sun's rays strike
    and focus the tiny branch
    tips of a small bush
    at a certain peculiar angle
    that shattered the blinders
    I've always worn
    and for an instant
    before my hooded sight
    surged back
    the bare world
    poured through
    my eyes

# August Harvest

For three hot August days now
I have been harvesting stones
with my bare hands.
With growing confidence
my eyes have scouted yard,
field, and pit for the no
more than three-inch thick
slabs that I must have.
My sore fingers have learned
to pry them from their earth
habitats, exposing their moist
underside to the plangent
light of day. The weight
of several big ones stacked
like primeval plates has
staggered me battling
gravity for hundreds of
feet upfield, the inertia
of their noiseless eons
pulling against my straining
back, thighs, knees. Like
a mere beast of burden I
have sweated their odd
shapes and sizes out of
the earth, have pushed
myself to the limit to
confound myself with nothing
more than matter. In losing
the difference between their
years and mine I have found
the hard sheerness of rock,
have felt alone at the base
of my spine the enduring
presence of stone.

# The Water Witch

*(in memory of Ray Tead)*

On the third day in the hideaway
house you bought in the Groveland
hills the old hand-dug farmwell
runs dry. It refuses to recover
as days turn into weeks: neither
prayers nor curses nor wholesale
hopes help in the least. So you
check out the local grapevine
for the best dowser. Since he
doesn't have a phone you drive
long miles over back roads to
find him in a falling-down house
in Conesus that looks like a
Northern version of Dogpatch.

The ageless water witch with his
cheek bulging with chewing tobacco
and rotten stumps for teeth and who
smells like he hasn't been in contact
with water for years scuttles through
the tall grass at dusk with his glossy
eyes and nose pointing up in the air
like a bird dog's on the scent.
The forked cherry stick rotates
between thumbs and forefingers
of his upturned hands. He is
scouting out the main veins
which a few minutes later
he will trace out on a pad
of paper along with scribbled
rows of tiny figures. When he
holds his battered wristwatch
over the center of what he claims
will be your well the second hand
stops dead in its tracks. He puts
your hand on his wrist and tells you
to grip it tight: you do, and with
a sudden exhilarating rush up your
spine you feel the downward pull
as the divining rod turns and turns
to the distant source in the cool

*Moving to the Country*

ground. He lets you feel his
palms still hot with friction.

The well is witched. After
calculating his figures at
the kitchen table he informs
you how much water—four to six
gallons per minute—how far down—
eighty feet—you will have. Don't
go over eighty, he cautions,
or you'll have egg water (meaning
sulfur). He adds that around May and
September 15 you'll have a touch
of it anyway. And then he tells
you the story of his life…
After you have paid him the agreed
on fee of twenty-five dollars, you
believe, and you do not believe.

The following week a sixty-eight
year old well-driller with a 1943
army surplus truck (same year as you)
sets up over the staked spot,
scoffing at water witches and
their misleading ways. He has
emphysema and had a heart attack
twenty years ago, but climbs on
his tall rig as nimbly as a monkey
and brings you pounds of cod he
caught on a fishing trip last
week to Gloucester. He hits
water at thirty feet and stops
at seventy-nine when he's getting
four gallons a minute. The water
man's prediction is pure coincidence,
he claims, and cheerfully informs
you that you do have sulfur. But
you're damn glad to have
whatever water's there.

After the well is hooked into
the house plumbing and the pipes
are flushed of mud and grit
the first glassful you hold up
to the light sparkles like
expensive crystal and tastes
better than any Perrier.

# Turning Forty

At forty one begins to learn to live with one's failures. I didn't say accept, for that would be to die, like a cactus taking its bare spines as the last word. No, no, I'm not ready for that yet. But of failures and shortcomings, o lord, how many, and how rife I am with them, how rich! To be sure, to be rich in defeats is in itself a sort of accomplishment, like being a veteran of arduous wars, like some eagle-tufted relic of an Indian chief displaying his cicatriced wounds years after his last battle has been fought—o those prides of failure, those loud brags, lord, keep me from these as well. Let them simply be—failures: no more, no less: as a poet, first and foremost, as a critic and a scholar, as a teacher, as a husband, as a son and brother, and over and above these fractured selves, as a human being. The poetry in me has almost died in the unstillable thirst to put myself in print, for god's sake, to get published at any cost, though this vanity has had some soothing lately in the newer knowledge that those too soon in print are too soon out of print, forgotten almost before they are known. And also, what an embarrassment to be known before one's time, before one's voice has found and formed itself, or worse yet, to be caught with one's sticky hands smack-dab in the poetic cookie-jar, filching sweets that cloy from various mouths that are not properly one's own, to be kissing the void air with others' made-up lips! At forty it also seems to me one should be able to write off early failures like early successes, to itemize and deduct them in the IRS of one's so careful conscience. O lord, let me be indifferent to my various stupid vanities, let me bide my time without ado and clamoring, let me be as a bear or a groundhog in winter, let me hug the earth even if the frolics of spring are never sprung for me, let me be rid of my goddammed ego, and, lord o lord, let me become that most impossible and difficult of simple things:

        merely myself.

# Inland

*("though inland far we be")*

My once infant feet are now
time-shod. It's been years
since my toes have touched
the sea. Inland so long
I've been that I've quite
forgotten there are such
things as shores. Those
mighty waters are the merest
lispings of memory in my
inner ear. This mainland
air's like dry ice on my
lame brain. I wouldn't
know how to stand on
point where the mountains
front the tide. Do they
ever? do any such geoscapes
exist save through the prism
of my dreams? Gradually
I've become aware of
everything I've failed
to become though I insist
that the sentence chiseled
on the wall is merely a
crazy stenciling on
flames (and may the flames
take all). Maybe if I stay
inland long enough the sea
will come to me—maybe an
artesian well will burst
like a geyser in my
discommoded garden, and
like some retired seal
returning to action I'll
plummet back to those
fabulous depths below
the flood: speechless
quite at feet splayed
to fins and arms be-
flippered, a sea-changed
me will glide down
aquamarine avenues
of amber light.

# Poet Marginal

I mouth the words that none
can hear in the margins of
this blind canvas of your
world. For sure you own
it, proud. Hanging by
nothing but a phrase from
your metal frame I need
no ears to hear, I need
no tongue to praise.
When like sharp cacti
spines my vexed vowels
slice holes in your no
show vistas you will
choke on my blood welling
up in your prim mouths,
your shredded tongues
stuttering sanguine
epitaphs. With a full
and sincere complicity
of silence my anemic
lips will seal themselves
to your frozen border.
Such chill margins
are intimately mine,
such dumb peace my
nowhere reward, waste
space and cacti spine
my only crave.

# About Trees

Trees make no demands
even on dogs nor do they
signal with their eyes.
To the despair of ships
and planes they straddle
the earth. With equal
ease and without ever
expressing a preference
they are turned into
firewood, houses, and
metaphors. Trees let
the wind speak with
itself; trees guard
firmly the secrets of
our early years.
Politicians do not
shake their branches
which vote only with
leaves. Trees do not
charge their tenants
rent nor do they talk
back to their spouses.
Trees have never fallen
from paradise; trees
can become poems but
poems naturally never
can be trees. Trees
know no resentment
but quietly harvest
the casual music
of the skies.

# Mimy Bird

I'm the ubiquitous Mimy Bird.
I'm equally at home in Hollywood,
any corporate headquarter, university
administration, or the White House.
I can fluff my feathers like yours,
tuft for tuft, or twist my beak
precisely into your scowl. My
head droops with yours, I can
front the gust just as you do.
I squat on the same powerline
in the rain, feather for feather.
I pick at the worms in the grass
peck for peck with you; when you
sleep, so do I; you wake, and
I do too. You think I'm only
your double when really I'm
your counterfeit self. You
rise, you soar; I rise, I
soar. You twitter, I twitter;
you build your nest, I build;
you mate, I mate alongside you,
tit for tat. I can even mime
myself, for I'm the ubiquitous
Mimy Bird.

# Middle Ages

In the Middle Ages they liked to think
of the World as a Book.
The Author was understood,
His intention explicit in every line.

Approaching middle age I too
like to think of the world
as a book.

We who are the print are none too
clear to me; there are lots of
typos, comma splices, misplaced
modifiers, sentence fragments,
and general redundancies just
as in the freshman themes I'm
condemned to read by the thousands
after having done an advanced
degree in Truth and Beauty.

There are blank pages too, and
missing chapters which challenge my
ingenuity: as for the Author and
Title, your guess is as good as
mine. The Table of Contents reads:
More of the Same. Index there
is none.

No library I can imagine could
house such a Text. There are
intermittent rumors that it
is long overdue and will be
recalled at any moment now.

# Appropriating the Land

Early autumn is rife again with
the hoarse groan of heavy farm
machinery. Familiar fields are
ripped open and tiled, dozers
smash down trees already sold
to loggers. Tons of earth are
shifted according to the neat
notions of cost-accounting minds.
No, mechanized modern farmers
nature do not love (nineteenth
century Wordsworth to the contrary)
save as it can reap quick
cash crops: nature's mostly
there to pay off heavy machinery.

A head with headphones attached
bops atop a monstrous combine,
the operator's mesmerized by the
fractious urban rhythms piped into
his ears as his huge ribbed wheels
criss cross criss cross acres he
neither sees nor knows. He's
the owner's son; it is or will
be his some day. And what, pray
tell, is ownership? What's whose,
and why? By what deed, title,
or right? Can our senses stake
out a claim, or do we own
what we own only with our
wallets and various pieces
of paper? Can mere love
establish title? If yes

then I'm the true owner of
these sloping conformations,
I and you who take their pulse
daily in our random rambles,
who cross these rolling hills
again and again in winter on
skis when they are void of
machinery, a mere wilderness

of windswept snow, who survey
all this through the seasons
with our senses and our souls,
who take their measure in our
stride and study their hazy lines,
who chronicle this world with our
hearts and take in their changing
appearances from the ash-yellow
cornstalks of late autumn to the
rain-sodden lowlands of first
spring. We are the true owners,
and so is our Afghan hound who
flows across the fields like
the wind, who marks her spots
and knows every foot of ground
by its particular scent, and even
more the deer hold it in perpetual
trust for the vanished redmen
in their shy glide between
the trees and their tail-high
bounding over fences; and the
lone-ranger raccoons own it who
stake out their claim at night
on the dirt roads frozen by the
headlights of our car, and the
darting chipmunks own it, and
the butterflies who ride and slide
upon the air, and the groundhogs
who make a fat waddling beeline for
the culvert, and the russet fox
whose brush whooshes across the
trail before you know it's been
there, and all that teeming life
owns it whose countless generations
inscribed their deeds in fur, bone,
feather, tooth and blood eons
before these flinty grasping
farmers sunk their metal fangs
into this ancient land to gouge
and spoil the scheme of things.

# Unless

Why can't I bear to even look at
any of the countless poems I've
written over two decades or so?
Fear of or indifference to the
grimacing faces of ghostly selves
in the elongating corridors of my
dim past? No, it's more likely that
my dreams have gone bust: the imperial
argosy of my dreams has apparently
foundered in a drawer full of dust.
Those terse rejection slips which
deck the walls of my private gallery
have become the scripture and tomb
of what I once aspired to be.
I've touched the graveled bottom
of poetry for so long that I've
quite forgotten that there are
such things as a broad expanse
of white sails merging with a
pastel sky or the cry of seabirds
fathoming the unstilled salt air.
And my ending is despair unless
I be relieved not by the kindly
regard of the readers I've never
had but by the quiet strength of
a sun-splayed summer rock, by
the simple prospect of the slim
tips of my crosscountry skis
bisecting the endless plane of
an upstate field with geometric
precision on a windy winter
afternoon, by the laughter of
friends or the subtle touch of
a loving hand, by the spirited
babble of a little child or
the shy glide of the bluebird
through the recumbent
summer wood.

# Paths

The undiscovered paths you haven't
traveled may lead you to
a clearing. Empty mouths don't
dare, chewing-gum teeth masticate
*the known*. All shortcuts have led
you far afield. The main road you
took is a by-pass that goes right
by. How to turn? Not like a weather-
vane spinning to prevailing gusts.
Making a few choice politicians
*sauter en l'air* (though perhaps
well-deserved), won't do: they're
only the symptom of the wrong
turn, the dead end, the ring road.
And bloody hands can't grasp
the light.

The conditional *may*
is only a grammatical pointing:
it doesn't guarantee anything,
only provides an opening to
the horizons of the possible—
of what may be, maybe.
Grammar is a slide zone, not
a word-screen: the launching
pad of the hypothetical, the
heuristic *what if*? And if there
is a clearing it's surely blocked
by megatons of advertising,
slick mindwarps (thanks bill blake)
of public relations that keep
us perpetually looking the other
way, goggle-eyes stuck in
the back of our head.

Positioned in language,
shifting foundations, how
to make a start? Placed by
words, why *not* proceed?
"What *if* the clearing is only
words?" whisper the demons.

Let them. All you know today
is that the paths you've
avoided are a clue, not
a key. Clues are there
to be pondered. The kinds
of clues you seek have no
solution but if you're willing
to track them all alone on
the paths of your heart they
may take you to the white light
of a clearing where you may
be in a position to begin
for the first time to ask
a real question, to find
no answer but to grab with
your own hands the terms of
a problem beyond all the
nostalgias of your past.

But first you have to uncover
the invisible paths you've never
hazarded, to see a subtle pleat
in the landscape of the completely
given, to hear the one false note
in the old song of yourself that
might set you on the right track.

That first first will be like
climbing up the rockface of
a frozen waterfall with your
bare hands and feet.

# Geneva Summit

1

Not too many weeks ago in Mexico City
a monstrous earthquake shook several thousand
people dead. Everybody wanted to help
in the desperate struggle to extricate
those pinned alive under tons of rubble.
The world's hopes hung on them,
dying only with the faint cries of
a helpless boy who never was found.

2

In dour Calvin's city by the romantic lake
they will preside in several days at the summit
of global superpower, Russkis and Amerikanskis
with their nuclear arsenals that hold the world
hostage in an overbalance of terror. Ad nauseam
they will talk Peace, yes Peace, only Peace,
by God and by Lenin, Peace, only and above all
Peace, but piece by piece they will continue
to heap up their weapons systems in a hypertrophy
of mutual fear and distrust which we captive
citizens of the world dare not even comprehend.
"Peace" they will say, these princes
of the world's darkness.

3

Communiques will be issued hour by hour
simultaneously in nearly all the world's
tongues, yet none of them will be "frank" or
"productive" or even bear the slightest
resemblance to human speech. And with peace
they will of course have nothing whatever
to do. O for a single human voice at that
death-dealing summit, o for the single syllable
of a Socrates, a Christ, a Lao-Tzu and so many
more true princes of peace who of course are
never heard at these sabbaths of power.

4

Last week in Colombia the volcano Nevado del Ruiz
burst through the roof of the sky and over twenty
thousand lost their lives in an apocalypse of
melted glacier ice and mud. Everybody who saw
the horrific images broadcast to the world
wanted to help: millions upon millions of hearts
went out to the homeless survivors in a primal
bond of human sympathy. Anything to help, where
even the best and quickest remedy can only be
too little and too late. For we citizens of
the world want only to help in spite
of all that terrible dying.

5

*Ich bin der Geist der stets verneint*:
A silent unseen partner smirking Mephisto sits
at the Geneva summit. He's well versed in
the inhuman lingo of the opposing leaders
and their handlers who despite their twisted
rhetoric are all of the same party as they pass
around a kind of AIDS of the mind. In his knowledge
that everything that has ever come into being is fit to
be destroyed Mephisto is the proper impresario of our
age of Nuclear Angst. He winks at the negotiators
as he hands them implements to sign meaningless
agreements; he cracks polyglot jokes with the
international claque of sycophant reporters, he drools
Peace and Mutual Understanding
after the two sides have conspired to continue
fueling their inveterate lusts and fears.

6

On the evening news the grief-etched face of a
Colombian *campesino* tells how his wife and children
were swept away before his eyes in the terrible flood.
I who hardly know Spanish know only too well
the meaning of his words. The tears on the mask
of his ferocious face speak plain enough to
the human heart, speak with awful power
to and for all of us frozen in the very impotence
of our good will. The final news image of the volcano's

horror is his ageless peasant's form dwarfed by an
ocean of mud. Swift and silent the television camera
cuts back to Geneva and the smug smiles of high-ranking
diplomats who toast each other's masks in full view of
the assembled paparazzi of power. Then as the public
relations cliches bubble into the champagned air to
the relentless clicking and flashing of cameras,
the Anusol commercial suddenly floods the screen.

# September Gifts

Out for a morning walk in the Groveland
hills I saw a two-inch baby salamander
cross the path in front of me. Because I
had never seen one before my mind reeled
at what magic had come my way: a gift of
the deep earth! a gift! So I stood solemn
guard at the crossing of this miniature
dragon lapped in unseen tongues of flame,
and wished it safe passage. So delicate
this smidgen of spotted crimson against
the moist brown earth, infinitesimal
spark of the starred firmament's fire,
frail life's first setting forth.
The burden of all being seemed to rest
on it as it felt its way to the other side
of the path with the assurance of the newly-
fledged who give themselves to the eternal
difference with the noblesse oblige of
ancient blood. Sure a sign this was
of what was to come whose meaning
I could not yet guess but whose promise
I must trust and honor. As a further
September pledge the following day
a falling leaf zig-zagged into my open
waiting hand: had I sought to grasp it
I never could have, but this nine-pointed
confirmation of the season danced toward me
on the very rhythm of the air and with
a perfect reflex my fingers closed on
all that fragile promise.

Made in the USA
Middletown, DE
29 September 2015